Asperger's Syndrome

of related interest

Children with Autism, Second Edition
Diagnosis and Interventions to Meet Their Needs
Colwyn Trevarthen, Kenneth Aitken, Despina Papoudi and Jacqueline Robarts
ISBN 1 85302 555 0

Autism: An Inside-Out Approach
An Innovative Look at the Mechanics of 'Autism' and Its Developmental 'Cousins'
Donna Williams
ISBN 1 85302 387 6

Autism and Sensing
The Unlost Instinct
Donna Williams
ISBN 1 85302 612 3

Children with Special Needs, Fourth Edition
Assessment, Law and Practice: Caught in the Acts
John Friel
ISBN 1 85302 460 0

Asperger's Syndrome
A Guide for Parents and Professionals

Tony Attwood

Jessica Kingsley Publishers
London and Philadelphia

Extract from *Notes from a Small Island* by Bill Bryson © 1995 B. Bryson. Published by Transworld Publishers Ltd. Reproduced by permission of William Morrow and Company, Inc., New York, and Greene and Heaton Ltd, London.

Extract from *Infantile Austism* by G. Bosch © 1970 G. Bosch. Reproduced by permission of Springer- Verlag Gmbh and Co. KG, Heidelberg.

Extract from 'Asperger's Syndrome – some epidemiological considerations: a research note' by C. Gillberg and I.C. Gillberg in the *Journal of Child Psychology and Psychiatry 30* © 1989 Association for Child Psychology and Psychiatry.

Extract from 'Exploring the experience of autism through first hand accounts' by L. Cessaroni and M. Garber in the *Journal of Autism and Development Disorders 21* © 1991 Plenum Publishing Corporation, New York.

Extract reprinted with permission from the *Diagnostic and Statistical Manual of Mental Disorders*, Fourth Edition © 1994 American Psychiatric Association.

Extract from *100 Training Games* by Gary Kroehnert © 1991 G. Kroehnert. Reproduced by permission of McGraw-Hill Book Company, Australia Pty Ltd.

First published in the United Kingdom in 1998 by
Jessica Kingsley Publishers Ltd
116 Pentonville Road
London N1 9JB, England
and
1900 Frost Road, Suite 101
Bristol, PA 19007, U S A

Second impression 1998
Third impression 1998
Fourth impression 1998

Copyright © 1998 Tony Attwood
Foreword Copyright © 1998 Lorna Wing

Library of Congress Cataloging in Publication Data
A CIP catalogue record for this book is available from the Library of Congress

British Library Cataloguing in Publication Data
Attwood, Tony
Asperger's syndrome: a guide for parents and professionals
1. Asperger's syndrome
I. Title
616.8'982

ISBN 1 85302 557 1

Printed and Bound in Great Britain by
Athenæum Press, Gateshead, Tyne and Wear

Contents

Acknowledgements

I would like to acknowledge the following for the encouragement, suggestions and support that has enabled me to acquire the knowledge and time to complete this book. Uta Frith and Lorna Wing are my heroes and have been an inspiration throughout my academic and clinical careers. My wife Sarah and our three children have continually been supportive and extraordinarily tolerant of my absence. The people I have met who have Asperger's Syndrome whose abilities and motives are often misunderstood; I hope this book will improve their circumstances. I admire many of their personal qualities and am proud such individuals are members of my family and friends. I am indebted to my professional colleagues for their ideas and comments, in particular Carol Gray, Brian Ross, Michelle Garnett and Judith Sheridan. Finally, the Asperger's Syndrome support network of Queensland and other parents who have provided positive criticism on the various revisions. I thank them for their encouragement that the book should be published. In answer to the many who have said, 'When will your book be available?' – here it is.

In memory of my grandmother, Elsie May Dovey
1903–1987

Foreword

People with Asperger's syndrome perceive the world differently from everyone else. They find the rest of us strange and baffling. Why don't we say what we mean? Why do we say so many things we don't mean? Why do we so often make trivial remarks that mean nothing at all? Why do we get bored and impatient when someone with Asperger's syndrome tells us hundreds of fascinating facts about time-tables, the individual numbers carved on lamp posts in the United Kingdom, the different varieties of carrots or the movements of the planets? Why do we tolerate such a confusion of sensations of light, sound, smell, touch and taste without getting to screaming pitch? Why do we care about social hierarchies – why not treat everyone in the same way? Why do we have such complicated emotional relationships? Why do we send and receive so many social signals to each other and how do we make sense of them? Above all, why are we so illogical compared to people with Asperger's syndrome?

The truth is, of course, that those with the syndrome are a small minority. The way they perceive the world makes sense to them and has some aspects that are admirable, but it often brings them into conflict with conventional (that is, majority) ways of thinking, feeling and behaving. They cannot change and many do not want to. However, they do need help in finding ways of adapting to the world as it is in order to use their special skills constructively, to engage in their special interests without coming into conflict with others and to achieve, as far as possible, some degree of independence in adult life and some positive social relationships.

Parents, other family members and professionals have to understand the point of view of people with Asperger's syndrome in order to work with them effectively. The strength of Tony Attwood's book is that he has made the essential imaginative leap into the Asperger world. He has real empathy with the children and adults he writes about, and his sympathy, knowledge and common sense come through on every page. Readers will appreciate the detailed discussions of the problems people with Asperger's syndrome will encounter and the practical suggestions for helping to overcome or compensate for them. This is a book to be read and consulted over and over again.

Lorna Wing

Preface

What is Asperger's Syndrome? A few years ago hardly anyone had heard of the term, yet today almost every school seems to have a child with this new syndrome. Yet the first definition of such children was published over 50 years ago by Hans Asperger, a Viennese paediatrician. He identified a consistent pattern of abilities and behaviour that predominantly occurred in boys. The pattern included a lack of empathy, little ability to form friendships, one-sided conversations, intense absorption in a special interest and clumsy movements. However, his pioneering work did not achieve international recognition until the 1990s. Until recently parents and teachers may have realised the child was unusual, but had no idea why, nor knew where to go for help.

I decided to write this book as a guide for parents and professionals to assist in the identification and treatment of children and adults with Asperger's Syndrome. It is a slim volume, which is a reflection of our current lack of knowledge, but it is based on an extensive review of the literature and my experience as a clinical psychologist specialising in this area. In the last 25 years I have met over a thousand individuals with this syndrome, ranging widely in age, ability and background, from children in pre-school to elderly people, including a retired professor who was awarded the Nobel Prize. I have always been impressed by their patience and ingenuity in achieving abilities others acquire without a second thought. I also applaud the parents and teachers who, despite the lack of resources and guidance, are able to obtain significant progress.

The book provides a description and analysis of the unusual characteristics, and practical strategies to reduce those that are most conspicuous or debilitating. There are numerous quotations from people with Asperger's Syndrome, as their insight and descriptions are clearer and more poignant than the text in scientific journals. I have also refrained from attempting to impress or confuse the reader with scientific terminology. I have always adopted the principle that if you cannot provide an explanation in simple terms, you do not understand what you are talking about. The reader does not require a postgraduate degree in psychology to translate the jargon, but for those who require further information I have included the original references.

Tony Attwood

CHAPTER I

Diagnosis

As the postman delivered the letters to Number 20, the young girl strode down the path towards him. The family had just moved in and he was curious as to the names and background of the new occupants. Before he could say good morning, she said 'Do you like Deltics?' Confused as to the relevance of such a question, the postman wondered whether a Deltic was a new chocolate bar or a character in a television programme. Before he could reply, she said, 'They are the most powerful diesel trains. The 2:30 from Kings Cross is a Deltic, I have 27 photographs of Deltics.' The postman was relieved to be enlightened about the subject matter of the conversation, but the relevance to him at that hour of the day was not immediately apparent. The girl proceeded to launch into a description of the qualities of this obscure locomotive. She was clearly not interested in his thoughts about such trains and appeared oblivious to his polite signals that he must get on with his rounds. Eventually he had to be quite blunt, interrupting her monologue with a sudden 'Goodbye' to make his escape. He was bewildered as to why this eccentric child was so knowledgeable about trains, and left thinking 'Why did she think I would be interested in trains? She hardly looked at me, and kept interrupting. Can't she talk about anything else? She was like a walking encyclopaedia.' This fictitious scene is typical of an encounter with a child with Asperger's Syndrome. A lack of social skills, limited ability to have a reciprocal conversation and an intense interest in a particular subject are the core features of this syndrome.

Parents may then explain how socially isolated the child is at school, having few genuine friends. They do not seem able to read people's body language, and may make comments that are true but potentially embarrassing. While waiting in the checkout line of a supermarket, the teenager loudly remarks of the person at the front of the queue, 'Isn't she big!'. When told quietly that you mustn't say that, replies at full volume, 'But she is really big!'. The cues that indicated the parent's embarrassment at the first comment are not recognised, nor the effect of both comments on the feelings of the lady in question. They are just confused as to why you disapprove of their comment when it is an accurate description of her size.

There is often a history of intense fascination with a special interest such as transport, animals or science. These interests come and go, but dominate the child's free time and conversation. There can be anecdotes where the child has taken a literal interpretation of a figure of speech, such as 'Has the cat got your tongue?', and an overprecise or pedantic quality to their speech. It is as if you were talking to a human dictionary. At school, teachers are aware of an uneven profile of abilities. The child may have remarkable long-term memory, exceptional concentration when engaged in their special interest and have an original method of problem solving. In contrast, there can be a lack of motivation and attention for activities that would enthral the others in the class, assessments that indicate specific learning difficulties, and motor clumsiness. There may also be some concern that the child is socially withdrawn in the classroom and playground, and prone to teasing by the other children. Thus both parents and teachers agree that this child who looks normal and has normal intellectual ability, for some inexplicable reason does not seem able to understand and relate to other people at the level one would expect for their age.

Lorna Wing was the first person to use the term Asperger's Syndrome in a paper published in 1981. She described a group of children and adults who had characteristics that very closely resembled the profile of abilities and behaviour originally described by the Viennese paediatrician, Hans Asperger. In his doctoral thesis, published in 1944, he described four boys who were quite unusual in their social, linguistic and cognitive (i.e. thinking) abilities. He used the term 'autistic psychopathy' to describe what he considered a form of personality disorder. It is interesting that he used the term 'autistic' as a fellow countryman, Leo Kanner, had just published in the United States another description of autistic children. Both authors described a similar pattern of symptoms and used the same term. Unfortunately, Hans Asperger's description was largely ignored in Europe and the United States for the next 30 years. However, he continued to see and treat children with autistic psychopathy. He started a remedial ward for such children and Sister Viktorine started the first educational programmes that involved speech therapy, drama and physical education. Tragically, she was killed when the ward was destroyed by allied bombing towards the end of the war, but Hans Asperger continued to be a highly regarded paediatrician (Frith 1991). He died in 1980, only a few years before the syndrome that bears his name achieved international recognition.

Both Leo Kanner and Hans Asperger described children with a poverty of social interaction, failure of communication and the development of special interests. Leo Kanner described children with a more severe expression of Autism, while Hans Asperger described more able children. However, Leo Kanner's work subsequently dominated our view of autism, such that the diagnostic criteria implied a conspicuous lack of responsiveness to other people and severe language impairments – the classic silent and aloof child. Lorna Wing was concerned that some children had the classic autistic features when very young, but developed fluent speech and a desire to socialise with others. On the one hand, they had progressed beyond a diagnosis of classic autism (according to the criteria based on Kanner's work); on the other hand, they still had significant problems with more advanced social skills and conversation. They more accurately resembled the original description by Hans Asperger.

Lorna Wing (Burgoine and Wing 1983) described the main clinical features of Asperger's Syndrome as:

- lack of empathy
- naive, inappropriate, one-sided interaction
- little or no ability to form friendships
- pedantic, repetitive speech
- poor non-verbal communication
- intense absorption in certain subjects
- clumsy and ill-coordinated movements and odd postures.

In the 1990s the prevailing view is that Asperger's Syndrome is a variant of autism and a Pervasive Developmental Disorder. That is, the condition affects the development of a wide range of abilities. It is now considered as a subgroup within the autistic spectrum and has its own diagnostic criteria. There is also evidence to suggest it is far more common than classic autism and may be diagnosed in children who have never previously been considered autistic.

The Diagnosis of Asperger's Syndrome

There can be two stages leading to a diagnosis of Asperger's Syndrome. The first involves parents or teachers completing a questionnaire or rating scale that can be used to indicate a child who might have the syndrome. The second stage is a diagnostic assessment by clinicians experienced in examining the behaviour and abilities of children with developmental disorders, using established criteria that give a clear description of the syndrome.

Stage 1: A rating scale

Few parents and frontline professionals, ie. teachers, therapists and general practitioners, have knowledge of the signs of Asperger's Syndrome and so may not consider that the child should be referred to a diagnostic service that specialises in Pervasive Developmental Disorders. Certainly the standard rating scales for autism are not designed for children with Asperger's Syndrome (Yirmiya, Sigman and Freeman 1993). Fortunately, two new rating scales have been developed to identify children at risk for this syndrome. They are designed for parents and teachers, the first being developed in Sweden (Ehlers and Gillberg 1993), the second in Australia (Garnett and Attwood 1995). They are based on the formal diagnostic criteria, the research literature on associated features and extensive clinical experience. The Australian Scale for Asperger's syndrome (or A.S.A.S.) is as follows.

AUSTRALIAN SCALE FOR ASPERGER'S SYNDROME

The following questionnaire is designed to identify behaviours and abilities indicative of Asperger's Syndrome in children during their primary school years. This is the age at which the unusual pattern of behaviour and abilities is most conspicuous. Each question or statement has a rating scale with 0 as the ordinary level expected of a child of that age.

A. SOCIAL AND EMOTIONAL ABILITIES

1. Does the child lack an understanding of how to play with other children? For example, unaware of the unwritten rules of social play.

   0 1 2 3 4 5 6
   Rarely   Frequently

2. When free to play with other children, such as school lunchtime, does the child avoid social contact with them? For example, finds a secluded place or goes to the library.

   0 1 2 3 4 5 6
   Rarely   Frequently

3. Does the child appear unaware of social conventions or codes of conduct and make inappropriate actions and comments? For example, making a personal comment to someone but the child seems unaware how the comment could offend.

   0 1 2 3 4 5 6
   Rarely   Frequently

4. Does the child lack empathy, ie. the intuitive understanding of another person's feelings? For example, not realising an apology would help the other person feel better.

   0 1 2 3 4 5 6
   Rarely   Frequently

5. Does the child seem to expect other people to know their thoughts, experiences and opinions? For example, not realising you could not know about something because you were not with the child at the time.

   0 1 2 3 4 5 6
   Rarely   Frequently

6. Does the child need an excessive amount of reassurance, especially if things are changed or go wrong?

   0 1 2 3 4 5 6
   Rarely   Frequently

7. Does the child lack subtlety in their expression of emotion? For example, the child shows distress or affection out of proportion to the situation.

   0 1 2 3 4 5 6
   Rarely   Frequently

8. Does the child lack precision in their expression of emotion? For example, not understanding the levels of emotional expression appropriate for different people.

   0 1 2 3 4 5 6
   Rarely   Frequently

9. Is the child not interested in participating in competitive sports, games and activities?

   0 1 2 3 4 5 6
   Rarely   Frequently

10. Is the child *indifferent* to peer pressure? For example, does *not* follow the latest craze in toys or clothes.

    0 1 2 3 4 5 6
    Rarely   Frequently

B. COMMUNICATION SKILLS

11. Does the child take a literal interpretation of comments? For example, is confused by phrases such as 'pull your socks up', 'looks can kill' or 'hop on the scales'.

```
0  1  2  3  4  5  6
L__I__I__I__I__I__J
Rarely        Frequently
```

12. Does the child have an unusual tone of voice? For example, the child seems to have a 'foreign' accent or monotone that lacks emphasis on key words.

```
0  1  2  3  4  5  6
L__I__I__I__I__I__J
Rarely        Frequently
```

13. When talking to the child does he or she appear uninterested in your side of the conversation? For example, not asking about or commenting on your thoughts or opinions on the topic.

```
0  1  2  3  4  5  6
L__I__I__I__I__I__J
Rarely        Frequently
```

14. When in a conversation, does the child tend to use less eye contact than you would expect?

```
0  1  2  3  4  5  6
L__I__I__I__I__I__J
Rarely        Frequently
```

15. Is the child's speech over-precise or pedantic? For example, talks in a formal way or like a walking dictionary.

```
0  1  2  3  4  5  6
L__I__I__I__I__I__J
Rarely        Frequently
```

16. Does the child have problems repairing a conversation? For example, when the child is confused, he or she does not ask for clarification but simply switches to a familiar topic, or takes ages to think of a reply.

```
0  1  2  3  4  5  6
L__I__I__I__I__I__J
Rarely        Frequently
```

C. COGNITIVE SKILLS

17. Does the child read books primarily for information, not seeming to be interested in fictional works? For example, being an avid reader of encyclopaedias and science books but not keen on adventure stories.

```
0  1  2  3  4  5  6
L__I__I__I__I__I__J
Rarely        Frequently
```

18. Does the child have an exceptional long-term memory for events and facts? For example, remembering the neighbour's car registration of several years ago, or clearly recalling scenes that happened many years ago.

```
0  1  2  3  4  5  6
L__I__I__I__I__I__J
Rarely        Frequently
```

19. Does the child lack social imaginative play? For example, other children are not included in the child's imaginary games or the child is confused by the pretend games of other children.

```
0  1  2  3  4  5  6
L__I__I__I__I__I__J
Rarely        Frequently
```

D. SPECIFIC INTERESTS

20. Is the child fascinated by a particular topic and avidly collects information or statistics on that interest? For example, the child becomes a walking encyclopaedia of knowledge on vehicles, maps or league tables.

0 1 2 3 4 5 6
Rarely   Frequently

21. Does the child become unduly upset by changes in routine or expectation? For example, is distressed by going to school by a different route.

0 1 2 3 4 5 6
Rarely   Frequently

22. Does the child develop elaborate routines or rituals that must be completed? For example, lining up toys before going to bed.

0 1 2 3 4 5 6
Rarely   Frequently

E. MOVEMENT SKILLS

23. Does the child have poor motor coordination? For example, is not skilled at catching a ball.

0 1 2 3 4 5 6
Rarely   Frequently

24. Does the child have an odd gait when running?

0 1 2 3 4 5 6
Rarely   Frequently

F. OTHER CHARACTERISTICS

For this section, tick whether the child has shown any of the following characteristics:

(a) Unusual fear or distress due to:

° ordinary sounds, e.g. electrical appliances ☐

° light touch on skin or scalp ☐

° wearing particular items of clothing ☐

° unexpected noises ☐

° seeing certain objects ☐

° noisy, crowded places, e.g. supermarkets ☐

(b) A tendency to flap or rock when excited or distressed ☐

(c) A lack of sensitivity to low levels of pain ☐

(d) Late in acquiring speech ☐

(e) Unusual facial grimaces or tics ☐

If the answer is yes to the majority of the questions in the scale, and the rating was between two and six (ie. conspicuously above the normal range), it does not automatically imply the child has Asperger's Syndrome. However, it is a possibility and a referral for a diagnostic assessment is warranted. Certainly, the remedial strategies described in subsequent chapters will still be relevant, as they explore each of the questions in the rating scale.

Stage 2: Diagnostic assessment

The diagnostic assessment takes at least an hour, and consists of an examination of specific aspects of social, language, cognitive and movement skills as well as qualitative aspects of the child's interests. There may also be some formal testing using a range of psychological tests. Time is also spent with the parents to obtain information regarding developmental history and behaviour in specific situations. Another invaluable source of information is reports from teachers and speech and occupational therapists.

During the diagnostic assessment, the clinician engineers situations to elicit specific behaviour and makes notes on a checklist of diagnostic signs. For example, when examining social behaviour a record is made of the quality of reciprocity, how the other person is included in the conversation or play, when eye contact would be anticipated, and range of facial expression and body language. The child is asked questions on the concept of friendship, and to identify and express a range of emotions. Parents are asked about the child's understanding of the codes of social conduct, response to peer pressure, degree of competitiveness, and their abilities when playing with other children. In a clinic environment it is usually not possible to observe the child's interactions with children of their age so a visit may be arranged to observe the child in their classroom and playground. Thus, there is a full assessment of their social skills.

There is also a distinct profile of language skills recorded with children with Asperger's Syndrome. The pattern often (but not always) includes a marginally late onset of speech, but when the child does learn to talk parents are exasperated by the incessant questioning and one-sided conversations. During the diagnostic assessment a record is made of errors in the pragmatic aspects of language, ie. how language is used in a social context. A common feature is that when the child is in doubt as to what to say in reply to a question during a conversation, they often fail to seek clarification, are reluctant to admit they don't know, can change to a topic they are familiar with or take ages to reply. There may be a fluent and advanced vocabulary but the choice of words is unusual, being somewhat pedantic or overly formal. There may be an odd tone of voice that is not consistent with other local children and an over-precise enunciation, for example pronouncing every letter in the word 'yes' when one may anticipate the vernacular, 'yeah'. A record is also made of incidents of the misuse of personal pronouns, e.g. using their Christian name rather than me or I, literal interpretation, and whether they vocalise their thoughts on occasions where they would be expected to be silent.

Cognitive, that is thinking and learning abilities, are also assessed. This includes a test of how well the child understands the thoughts and feelings of others using a series of stories. A note is also made of the child's choice in reading, their long-term memory for details and trivia, and the quality of their imaginative play, both as a solitary and social activity. Information from teachers and formal assessment of intellectual functioning is also extremely valuable.

The child's special interests are explored by examining whether they are typical of children of that age, their dominance in conversation and free time, and the type and history of interests. Parents are also asked about the child's reaction to changes in routine, imperfection, chaos and criticism.

Movement skills are also examined and the child is encouraged to catch and kick a ball, run, draw and write. A record is also made of any odd hand mannerisms or rocking, especially when happy or stressed, involuntary tics or twitches and grimaces. The parents are also asked to describe any unusual sensitivity to sound, touch and the texture or taste of food, as well as the degree of sensitivity to low levels of pain or discomfort. Finally, the clinicians examine the child for any signs of anxiety, depression or Attention Deficit Disorder, and whether there have been any similar children on either side of the family. A note is also made of any significant medical events during pregnancy, birth or infancy. It must be emphasised that none of the diagnostic characteristics of Asperger's syndrome are unique and it is unusual to find a child who has a severe expression of every characteristic. Each child is an individual in terms of the degree of expression in each of the areas.

For the clinician, it is essential to consider alternative diagnoses and explanations. Social withdrawal and immature social play can be a secondary consequence of a language disorder. Certainly Semantic Pragmatic Language Disorder (SPLD) has common features to Asperger's Syndrome. Young children with specific learning problems and developmental delay can also develop unusual social behaviour and one must consider whether the profile of abilities and behaviour is consistent with the child's developmental level. Children with an IQ within the superior range can consider social play as boring, acquire considerable knowledge in specific areas and appear eccentric, yet their profile of social and linguistic skills is within the normal range and not the same as occurs with Asperger's Syndrome. Children with Attention Deficit Disorder (ADD) are often considered as having some characteristics indicative of Asperger's Syndrome. Although they are two distinct disorders, they are not mutually exclusive and a child could have both conditions. One must undertake a very close examination of a range of skills and behaviour to discriminate between them. One must also consider the normal range of interpersonal skills and the characteristics of naturally shy, introvert or anxious children.

The differential diagnosis of other conditions similar to or associated with Asperger's Syndrome is discussed in Chapter 8. Suffice it to say at this point that the diagnostic process involves examining a range of explanations and alternative developmental disorders that may account for the signs that appear to indicate Asperger's Syndrome. The final part of the process is to apply the information obtained in the diagnostic assessment to the formal diagnostic criteria.

Diagnostic Criteria

Neither Hans Asperger nor Lorna Wing explicitly stated the criteria for diagnosis and at present there is no universal agreement on diagnostic criteria. Clinicians have a choice of four sets of criteria, two developed by organisations, two by clinicians. The most restrictive and stringent criteria are provided by the World Health Organisation in their tenth edition of the *International Classification of Diseases* and the American Psychiatric Association's fourth edition of their *Diagnostic and Statistical Manual of Mental Disorders*. The least restrictive are those criteria by Peter Szatmari and colleagues from Canada, and the criteria of Christopher and Corina Gillberg from Sweden. A copy of each set of criteria is provided in the Appendix. Which criteria to use is a matter of opinion, the present author preferring to use the criteria of the Gillbergs because they are clear, concise and comprehensive.

Six Pathways to Diagnosis

Recent research indicates the mean age for a diagnosis is eight years, but the age range varies from very young children to adults (Eisenmajer *et al.* 1996). The author has spent many years specialising in the diagnosis and treatment of children and adults with Asperger's Syndrome and there appear to be six pathways to diagnosis. The first is having a previous diagnosis of autism. This may have occurred when the child was less than two years old.

1. Diagnosis of autism in early childhood

One of the reasons why Lorna Wing proposed a wider acceptance of the term Asperger's Syndrome was the recognition that a proportion of children who had the classic signs of autism in their pre-school years may show significant improvement in communication and abilities. The previously withdrawn and severely language-impaired child develops fluent speech and the ability for supported inclusion in an ordinary classroom. They are no longer aloof and silent and their behaviour and abilities are consistent with a diagnosis of Asperger's Syndrome (Ozonoff, Rogers and Pennington 1991). This improvement can be remarkably rapid and occur just before the age of five (Shah 1988). We are not sure if this is a natural phenomenon for some children or a tribute to early intervention programmes; probably both. Nevertheless, the previous diagnosis of classic autism was accurate when the child was very young, but the child has progressed along the autistic continuum to the expression we call Asperger's Syndrome. Thus it is essential that the diagnosis of autism is regularly reviewed to examine whether

Asperger's Syndrome is now a more accurate diagnosis and the child should receive appropriately designed services.

2. Recognition of features when first enrolled at school

The child's development in the pre-school years may not have been conspicuously unusual, and parents or professionals may never have considered that the child had any features suggesting autism. However, the child's first teacher is familiar with the normal range of behaviour and abilities in young children and becomes concerned that the child avoids social play, does not understand the codes of social conduct in the classroom, has unusual qualities to their conversation and imaginative play, an intense fascination with a particular topic, and clumsiness when drawing, writing or playing with a ball. They can also be disruptive or aggressive when in unavoidable proximity to other children, or having to wait. At home, the child may be almost a different character, playing with siblings and interacting in a relatively natural way with their parents. In unfamiliar circumstances, however, and with their age peers, the signs are more apparent. These children have the classic signs but are often not considered by teachers as a priority for referral to diagnostic agencies. They are viewed as odd children, continuing through school and leaving each of their teachers perplexed.

A recent study in Sweden used a rating scale designed for teachers to identify children in their class who may have Asperger's Syndrome. Such children then underwent a diagnostic assessment using the standard criteria. It was originally thought that the incidence of Asperger's Syndrome was about one in a thousand children, a similar incidence to autism. But this study indicated the true incidence of Asperger's Syndrome to be around one in 300 children (Ehlers and Gillberg 1993). Thus the majority of children with this Syndrome will not have had a prior diagnosis of autism.

3. An atypical expression of another syndrome

The child's early development and abilities may have been recognised as unusual and examination suggests a particular disorder. For example, the child may have had a history of delayed language development, received treatment from a speech therapist and simply been assumed to have a language disorder. However, careful observation of the child's social and cognitive abilities and range of interests suggests the profile is more complex and Asperger's Syndrome is a more accurate diagnosis. The child may have received a diagnosis of Attention Deficit Disorder and this one condition is assumed to explain all features. Sometimes another condition is easily recognised, such as cerebral palsy or neurofibromatosis. Although the clinicians may be concerned that the child has an atypical expression, they are not sufficiently knowledgeable about Asperger's Syndrome to consider this a possibility. Eventually a clinician does recognise the signs or parents read about the syndrome and contact the relevant diagnostic team. Thus when one diagnosis is made, this does not exclude the possibility of another condition such as Asperger's Syndrome, and clinical experience and research studies have identified children with a dual diagnosis. However, parents may have to wait many years for the second diagnosis.

4. Diagnosis of a relative with autism or Asperger's Syndrome

When a child is diagnosed as having autism or Asperger's Syndrome, their parents soon become knowledgeable in the different ways these conditions are expressed. Such information is obtained from literature and conversations with professionals and other parents in the local support group. The question can then arise as to whether another member of the family could have Asperger's Syndrome. There are families with more than one child with Asperger's Syndrome or where the condition occurs in several generations.

5. A secondary psychiatric disorder

The person with Asperger's Syndrome may have progressed through the primary school years as a somewhat eccentric or reclusive child, but not have any signs that would indicate referral for a diagnostic assessment. However, as a teenager the person may become more aware of their social isolation and try to become more sociable. Their attempts to join in the social activities of their peers are met with ridicule and exclusion, causing the person to be depressed. The depression can lead to a referral to a child psychiatrist, who quickly becomes aware that this is a secondary consequence of Asperger's Syndrome.

Many young adults with Asperger's Syndrome report intense feelings of anxiety, and this may reach a level where treatment is required. The person may develop panic attacks or compulsive behaviour such as repeatedly having to wash their hands for fear of contamination. When these are diagnosed and treated, the clinicians involved can be the first to recognise signs of Asperger's Syndrome.

During adolescence, the person may retreat into their own inner world, talking to themselves and losing interest in social contact and personal hygiene. There may be a suspicion that they are developing schizophrenia, but careful examination reveals their behaviour is not psychotic, but an understandable reaction to Asperger's Syndrome during adolescence. These secondary psychiatric disorders, their prevention and treatment will be discussed in Chapter 8, but for some individuals they may be the signs that lead to the diagnosis of the syndrome.

6. Residual Asperger's Syndrome in an adult

Now that we are more aware of the nature of Asperger's Syndrome, referrals are not exclusively for children or adolescents. Some adults are referring themselves for a diagnostic assessment. They may be the parent or relative of a child who has had a diagnosis and consider that some of the features were apparent in their own childhood. Others have read about the syndrome in magazines or newspaper articles and consider they may have an expression of this syndrome. When conducting a diagnostic assessment of adults, it is very important to obtain reliable information on the person's abilities and behaviour as a child. Parents, relatives or teachers can be a source of invaluable knowledge to support the adult's recollections of their childhood.

There are also occasions when adult psychiatric services have eventually identified the signs in a person with an original diagnosis of atypical schizophrenia, or alcoholism. The incidence of schizophrenia among people with Asperger's Syndrome is similar to the incidence in the general population, but the signs in some individuals can be superficially similar, leading to a misdiagnosis. Sometimes alcoholism is a sign of depression or an attempt to reduce anxiety in social situations

– a form of Dutch courage. When the person receives treatment for alcoholism they are also diagnosed as having Asperger's Syndrome.

There have been extremely rare occasions when a person with Asperger's Syndrome has committed a criminal offence, often in relation to their special interest. For example, one young man was fascinated by trains and while on a station platform decided to 'steal' a railway engine. There was considerable doubt that he had any malicious intent; he was just over-enthusiastic and curious. Thus, forensic psychiatric services may refer the person for a diagnostic assessment. Finally, some government employment agencies are becoming aware of the special employment needs of those with a severe expression of the syndrome, and their professional staff may refer the person for diagnosis and advice on careers and employment support.

In summary, there are six pathways to diagnosis. Irrespective of whether the child or adult you are concerned about has a confirmed diagnosis, the following chapters will provide more information on the characteristics of the syndrome, and strategies to learn certain skills that are acquired so easily by others but have to be learnt by the person with Asperger's Syndrome.

CHAPTER 2

Social Behaviour

To a great extent, society appraises an individual by the way they look, behave and talk. The person with Asperger's Syndrome has no distinguishing physical features but is primarily viewed by other people as different because of their unusual quality of social behaviour and conversation skills. For example, a woman with Asperger's Syndrome described how as a child she saw people moving into the house across the street, ran up to one of the new kids and, instead of the conventional greeting and request of 'Hi, you want to play?', proclaimed, 'Nine times nine is equal to 81' (Schopler and Mesibov 1992). The eccentric social behaviour of such individuals can be remarkably conspicuous.

Diagnostic Criteria Relevant to Social Behaviour

The diagnostic criteria attempt to define the unusual profile of abilities and behaviour characteristic of Asperger's Syndrome, and all criteria refer to impaired social behaviour.

In 1989, Carina and Christopher Gillberg outlined six criteria, based on their studies in Sweden, and two of these describe aspects of social behaviour. The first criterion is titled Social Impairment, with the child having at least two of the following:

(a) inability to interact with peers

(b) lack of desire to interact with peers

(c) lack of appreciation of social cues

(d) socially and emotionally inappropriate behaviour.

Another of their criteria explores non-verbal communication but also reflects impairments in social behaviour in that the child has at least one of the following:

(a) limited use of gestures

(b) clumsy/gauche body language

(c) limited facial expression

(d) inappropriate expression

(e) peculiar, stiff gaze.

In the same year, Peter Szatmari and colleagues from Canada published their diagnostic criteria, and unusual qualities of social behaviour are described in three of their five criteria (Szatmari, Brenner and Nagy 1989). They emphasise several aspects that are not specifically addressed in the Gillbergs' criteria, namely being detached from or having difficulty sensing the feelings of others; not looking at others; the inability to 'give messages with their eyes'; and coming too close to others. The young child is less aware of the concept of personal space, and when this is encroached, the degree of discomfort. The World Health Organisation published their diagnostic criteria for Asperger's Syndrome in 1990. They stress that the child's social play can lack a mutual sharing of interests, activities and emotions and the modulation of behaviour according to the social context. The most recent criteria were published in 1994 by the American Psychiatric Association in their fourth edition of the *Diagnostic and Statistical Manual of Mental Disorders*. Their first criterion is a qualitative impairment in social interaction that includes many of the features described in previous criteria, but adds that the child may lack social and emotional reciprocity. In other words, the child can dominate the interaction. As we develop our knowledge of the unusual aspects of the social behaviour associated with Asperger's Syndrome, the diagnostic criteria will become more precise. At this stage much of that knowledge is based on clinical impressions rather than rigorous scientific study. However, the following sections will provide more detail based on observations of how the child is different in a social context and what can be done to reduce those differences.

Play with Other Children

In Hans Asperger's original papers, he describes how the child does not join in with others and may even panic if forced to participate in a group (Asperger 1991). The young child with Asperger's Syndrome does not seem motivated or know how to play with other children of their age so that they are 'in tune' with the social activity. They seem quite content with their own company. Sula Wolff (1995) quotes a child who said:

> I just can't make friends ... I'd like to be on my own and look at my coin collection ... I've got a hamster at home. That's enough company for me... I can play by myself. I don't need other people. (p.7)

They are more self-centred than selfish. Some may be observers on the periphery of social play or prefer to be with much younger or older children. When involved in joint play, there can be a tendency to impose or dictate the activity. Social contact is tolerated as long as the other children play their game according to their rules. Sometimes social interaction is avoided not simply because of a lack of social play skills, but because of a desire to have complete control over the activity. This is illustrated by Donna Williams' (1992) description of her childhood:

> Kay was from my neighbourhood. She was probably the most popular girl in our year. She'd line up her friends and say: 'You're my first best friend; you're my second best ...'. I was twenty-second. A quiet Yugoslavian girl was last. I was pretty, I was cheerful and sometimes I was entertaining, but I did not know how to play *with* children. At most, I knew how to create very simple games or adventures and sometimes allow others to participate, as long as it was totally on my terms. (p.24)

To include other children is to risk an alternative script, interpretation or conclusion – that is, you have to share and cope with different ideas. The child is not interested in doing the activities other children want to do and is not inclined to explain what they are doing. The child appears to play in a 'bubble' and can resent other children intruding into their activity. When the child intends to play on their own and other children are inquisitive or want to be sociable, they can be quite abrupt or even aggressive in ensuring their solitude. They often prefer to be left alone to continue their activity uninterrupted.

At school lunchtimes the child is often found on their own in a secluded area of the playground, sometimes talking to themselves or in the library reading about their particular interest. One child, when asked why he did not talk to other children in the playground, replied, 'No thank you. I don't have to.' There is a strong preference to interact with adults who are far more interesting, knowledgable and more tolerant and accommodating of their lack of social awareness.

The child does not see themselves as a member of a particular group and follows their own interest rather than that of the other children in the playground or class. They are often not interested in competitive sports or team games. For example, during a game of rounders (a cross between cricket and baseball) the child with Asperger's Syndrome was able to bat and bowl as well as the other members of his team. When a team mate was running, all the others cheered and jumped with excitement to encourage his success. But the child with Asperger's Syndrome remained still and without emotion as he was distracted by a butterfly. He had no interest in the success of his team. An adolescent with Asperger's Syndrome described how he was unable to appreciate the feeling of triumph in team sports as he could not comprehend how or why one would have a sense of satisfaction in knowing that your opponents felt inferior.

The child can be indifferent to peer pressure for the latest toys or clothes, is rarely invited to parties and has few genuine friends. Younger children can become indifferent to such isolation, content to play by themselves or with brothers and sisters. Older children become aware of their isolation and, in time, are genuinely motivated to socialise with children of their age. However, it becomes apparent that their social play skills are immature and rigid and they are often rebuffed by other children. This is perhaps one of the saddest moments for parents.

Codes of Conduct

The child with Asperger's Syndrome does not seem to be aware of the unwritten rules of social conduct and will inadvertently say or do things that may offend or annoy other people. The child may use true but potentially embarrassing personal comments – for example, a teenager with Asperger's Syndrome suddenly stopping in mid-conversation to observe loudly on the crookedness of the other person's teeth. An accurate observation, perhaps, but not a comment that encourages a smooth flow in the conversation. Another child, fascinated by computers, overheard a conversation between his parents that included the information that the neighbours had a new computer. He immediately entered their house and started to use the new machine. The problem was that this was after 11.00p.m. and the neighbours were in bed. He was quite perplexed as to why they would first be anxious that there might be an intruder downstairs, and then angry that he had not sought their consent.

Once codes of conduct are explained then the child often rigidly enforces them, perhaps becoming the class policeman, honest to a fault when such behaviour actually breaks the code of conduct. For example, in class the teacher was distracted and a child was deliberately misbehaving to the delight of the other children. The teacher realised someone had just been disobedient and asked, 'Who did that?' There was a long silence, broken by the child with Asperger's Syndrome who helpfully announced who had misbehaved, unaware of the glares of disapproval from the other children as he had broken the code of silence. Other children are determined to bend or break the rules, but the child with Asperger's Syndrome is intent on enforcing them.

On occasions the person may appear ill-mannered; for example, one young man with Asperger's Syndrome wanted to attract his mother's attention while she was talking to a group of her friends, and loudly said, 'Hey, you!', apparently unaware of more appropriate means of addressing his mother in public. The child, being impulsive and not aware of the consequences, says the first thing that comes into their mind. Strangers may consider the child to be rude, inconsiderate or spoilt, giving the parents a withering look and assuming the unusual social behaviour is a result of parental incompetence. They may comment, 'Well, if I had him for two weeks he would be a different child.' The parents' reaction may be that they would gladly let them have the child, as they need a rest, and to prove a point. It is essential that other people understand that the child is not being rude, but did not know a more tactful alternative or appreciate the effect on other people.

Carol Gray (in press) has developed a technique called Social Stories that is proving remarkably effective in enabling the child to understand the cues and actions for specific social situations. It also enables others to understand the perspective of the child, and why their social behaviour can appear naive, eccentric or disobedient. Events will have occurred where the child's behaviour in a social situation does not conform to the anticipated codes of conduct. The technique involves creating a short story that describes the situation and includes appropriate actions and expressions. For example, the child may have been reported to their teacher for disruptive behaviour in the line or queue for school lunches. The initial explanation may be that the child is being deliberately irresponsible, aggressive or rude. These may be explanations appropriate to other children, but the first stage in the technique is to consider the situation from the perspective of the child with Asperger's Syndrome. Conversation with the child about the event may reveal that they are confused as to the reasons for lining up for lunch, why they have to form a line, where to join the line and how to behave when waiting. These aspects are taken for granted with other children, but one cannot make these assumptions with a young child who has Asperger's Syndrome. They often seem to lack what could be called social common sense. However, they can learn what to do if someone provides an explanation.

By creating a short story, the situation is described in terms of relevant social cues, anticipated actions and information on what is occurring, and why. The stories are written according to specific guidelines based on Carol's extensive use of this technique. There is a ratio of four types of sentences, namely:

Descriptive: objectively define where a situation occurs, who is involved, what they are doing and why

Perspective: describe, and explain if necessary, the reactions and feelings of others in a given situation

Directive: state what the child is expected to do or say

Control: develop strategies to help the person remember what to do or how to understand the situation. These are often suggested and written by the child themselves and can incorporate their special interest.

There needs to be a balance of these four types of sentences, avoiding too many directives and too few descriptive and perspective sentences. Carol recommends a ratio of 0–1 directive and/or control sentence for every 2–5 descriptive and/or perspective sentences. Otherwise the story becomes a list of what to do without explaining when or why. The vocabulary must be appropriate for the child's age, reading comprehension and attention span. The stories are usually written in the first person and present tense as though they are describing events for the child as they take place. This personalises the content and avoids problems with time perception and syntax. The initial story can describe a situation where the child is already successful so they can first concentrate on learning the rules of the game. The story for a pre-school child will contain few large words per page and include photographs or illustrations. Pre-readers can listen to the story on an audiotape. Parents and teachers of older children can prepare the story as if they are a journalist, using the language and graphics of a newspaper or magazine article. For example, an article can be written on the codes of conduct between friends or what to do and say when approaching a classmate while shopping with parents.

The following is an example of a Social Story relevant to one of the situations described above, namely a young child being reported for disruptive behaviour while waiting in line for lunch.

My school has many rooms (descriptive). One room is called the lunch room (descriptive). Usually the children eat lunch in the lunch room (descriptive). The children hear the lunch bell (perspective). The children know the lunch bell tells them to line up at the door (perspective). We have a line to be fair to those who have waited there longest (perspective). As each person arrives they join the end of the line (directive). When I arrive I will try to join the end of the line (directive). The children are hungry. They want to eat (perspective). I will try to stand quietly in the lunch line until it is my turn to buy my lunch (directive).

Lunch lines and turtles are both very slow (control). Sometimes they stop, sometimes they go (control). My teacher will be pleased that I have waited quietly (perspective).

This story has been customised for the individual and their circumstances. This child has a special interest in reptiles so a key part of the text has particular relevance to him. The word 'usually' was deliberately chosen as there can be variations as to where lunch is eaten. The word 'try' was also chosen to emphasise that we are not expecting perfection every time. The words 'sometimes' and 'probably' can also be used to avoid a literal interpretation and enable the child to accommodate changes in routine and expectation. Thus the creation of Social Stories is an ingenious technique for ensuring the child understands the reasons and cues for the codes of conduct that are so important in our lives.

Gradually the child with Asperger's Syndrome learns the codes of social conduct, more by intellectual analysis and instruction than natural intuition. They have to think hard what to do. Indeed, one can sometimes observe the child taking time to think what he should do or say when other children respond immediately, that is, without a second thought; for the child with Asperger's Syndrome, thought is very necessary. The next section outlines some strategies that encourage the acquisition of other social behaviours that are impaired.

Programmes for Appropriate Social Behaviours

What can parents do?

The first stage is to observe the social games and activities being played by children of a similar age and to play with the child, practising these games. If the most popular social games for boys at the school are playing with balls and toy cars, then practise catching and ball skills and imaginative play with cars. The idea is not only to improve competence with the activity, but to model what is supposed to be said and done, and how to include the other person. Sometimes even the most basic rules have to be explained, for example, that you only pass the ball to people in your team, despite the requests of your opponents. Thus, basic and specific play skills will need to be taught. However, other children may not have the tolerance to play with a child with Asperger's Syndrome, so it is important for the child's parent to become their best friend and play with them as if they were a child of that age. This is an opportunity for an adult to legitimately revert to childlike behaviour. Go ahead and play on the adventure playground, build train tracks, make mud pies and play chasing games – remember, you have the patience and understanding to play with your son or daughter and to encourage them to learn what to do.

The next stage is to observe the child when playing with other children and make a note of specific skills that will have to be taught. Some of the common ones are:

○ *How to start, maintain and end the play*
The child may have to learn to say 'Can I join in?' 'What would you like to do next?' 'Can you help me?' or 'I want to play by myself now'. Otherwise, the child may blatantly state the obvious, as in the comment 'You won't do what I say – I don't want to play with you', being unaware that such comments do not encourage friendships.

○ *Flexibility, cooperation and sharing*
The child with Asperger's Syndrome may want to take total control of the activity and not tolerate any alternative suggestions or want to include other children. It is important to explain that the activity is not 'wrong' if conducted in a different way, and can be completed in less time with a better result when sharing equipment and ideas.

○ *How to avoid social play*
When the child wants to play alone, it may be necessary to teach comments and actions that are socially acceptable. The child may be labelled as aggressive but observation reveals that he or she has simply learnt that such behaviour ensures isolation. The child is not being aggressive for dominance or to acquire possessions. Once an appropriate phrase has been taught, it is also important that other children are encouraged to comply with their request.

○ *Explain what you should have done*
Errors in social behaviour are due to several factors, in particular not understanding the consequences on the feelings of others, and being unaware of what they are supposed to do or a more appropriate or subtle alternative. Rarely does such behaviour have malicious intent.

Remember, always explain what the child should have done and ask them to think how the other person may feel as a consequence of what they say or do.

○ *Invite a friend to the house*
Invite a potential friend to visit. Ensure the occasion is a success, perhaps by arranging an outing and ensuring an adult plays with the children to minimise the influence of the child's limited social play skills. An enjoyable time may ensure that an invitation to return is accepted.

○ *Enrol the child in clubs*
School may provide the only occasions for social play but social experiences can be extended by joining clubs such as Scouts. The advantage of these activities is that they are usually supervised and structured. Parents will need to explain the nature of the child's problems to the adult in charge and strategies they have found to be successful.

What can the teacher do?

The classroom provides an opportunity to learn a range of appropriate social behaviour for the child with Asperger's Syndrome. The following are some strategies:

○ *Use other children as cues to indicate what to do*
The child may be disruptive or intrusive as they are not aware of the codes of conduct for the classroom. When errors occur, remember to ask the child to first look at what the other children are doing – for example, sitting still, working silently or waiting in an orderly line. Inform the child that what they must do is observe the other children and copy what they are doing, assuming what they are doing is appropriate.

○ *Encourage cooperative games*
There is a range of classroom activities that involve small groups of children working as a team. The child may need supervision and guidance on turn taking, allowing others a fair opportunity and incorporating their suggestions. One problem can arise in competitive

games with the child with Asperger's Syndrome always wanting to be first. This may not be due to a desire to be superior but to have consistency in the order of participants, to know their position and personal satisfaction in success.

○ *Model how to relate to the child*
Other children in the class are often unsure how to react to the child's unusual social behaviour. They will look to the teacher as their first model. Therefore it is essential that the teacher demonstrates tolerance, tuition in social skills and encouragement, as their approach will be amplified within the classroom. It is also important to recognise and acclaim occasions when classmates are particularly supportive.

○ *Explain alternative means of seeking help*
The young child can consider the teacher as the only source of knowledge and assistance. It is important to explain that when a problem arises, help can be requested and obtained from other children rather than always referring to the teacher.

○ *Encourage prospective friendships*
Every child in the classroom has their own personality and it may take considerable time for the child with Asperger's Syndrome to learn how to interact with each one. It may help initially to identify and encourage interaction with a restricted number of children who are keen to help the child learn how to play with them. At this stage it does not matter if the friends are boys or girls. If prospective friends are identified, try to encourage the contact in the classroom and playground. They may become their guardians when teased or bullied by children from other classes. They are likely to include them in their games, act as their advocate in the classroom, and remind or instruct the person on what to do or say when the teacher is not available. It is remarkable how supportive and tolerant some young children can be.

○ *Provide supervision at break times in the playground*
For most ordinary children, the best time in the school day is free play in the playground. However, a lack of structure and supervision

and an atmosphere of intense socialising and noise is often not enjoyable for the child with Asperger's Syndrome. At this time they are at their least skilled and most vulnerable. The playground supervisors will need to know the difficulties faced by the child and encourage their inclusion or respect their need for solitude. The person may also be vulnerable while travelling on transport to and from school and need supervision during these times.

○ *Be aware of two characters*
The child may be very conscious of the necessity to follow the codes of conduct in the classroom and to try to be inconspicuous and behave like the other children. This pressure to conform and retain self control can lead to enormous emotional tension which, like a compressed spring, is released when the child reaches home. Here the child is a different character, almost a Jekyll and Hyde. This is a feature of some children with Asperger's Syndrome and not necessarily an indication of the parents being unable to manage their child. It will help for the classroom teacher to have a range of relaxing or solitary activities for the child just before they return home. Parents may also consider a period of relaxation or energetic activities when the child comes home to dissolve their tension from a long day at school.

○ *Teacher aide time*
As many of the skills outlined in this book are rarely taught as specific components of the school curriculum, it is essential that the young child with Asperger's Syndrome has access to a teacher aide to facilitate individual and small group tuition to improve social behaviour. The amount of hours necessary depends on the child, but the aide will require guidance on the nature of Asperger's Syndrome and remedial programmes. Further details on the value of a teacher aide are provided on page 171. If there are insufficient financial resources for an aide, then a child from a more senior grade can be a 'buddy' or aide as part of their humanities or citizenship course.

Social Skills Groups

There has been some success reported in the research literature for social skills groups for adolescents with Asperger's Syndrome (Marriage, Gordon and Brand 1995; Mesibov 1984; Ozonoff and Miller 1995; Williams 1989). These groups provide an opportunity to learn and practise a range of advanced social abilities. They can be a component of speech and drama classes at a high school or a separate programme run by specialists in Asperger's Syndrome. The group may comprise adolescents with Asperger's Syndrome who attend different schools and benefit from including several ordinary children. The number of participants in the group must be small to allow for individual tuition and minimal disruption. Prior to the sessions, group members, their teachers and families suggest examples of occasions when more advanced social skills would have been an advantage. Thus, a profile is prepared on strengths and weaknesses for each participant. It is also important to examine these occasions in some detail. This is to determine the person's perception and interpretation of the event, signals, motives and options. We acknowledge that people with Asperger's Syndrome may not fully understand the thoughts and feelings of others in a social context, but equally, we may not fully understand their thoughts and feelings.

The following are suggestions for activities within the groups:

○ Replay actual events where the person was unsure of alternative actions or comments, or misread the cues; then rehearse more appropriate options that are suggested by the participants.

○ Demonstrate inappropriate social behaviour and ask individuals to identify the errors. The group leader portrays someone who is extremely socially inept and the participants have to identify the errors. Gradually the errors become more subtle.
Illustrations can be used from video (*Mr Bean, The Brittas Empire* are an excellent source). Also acting what *not* to do can be great fun for the participants before demonstrating social competence.

○ An informal test of social reasoning has been developed for adolescents with Asperger's Syndrome by Margaret Dewey (1991), and by Hadyn Ellis and colleagues (1994). This is an excellent source of examples relevant to people with Asperger's Syndrome. The following are two illustrations.

> Charlie, age 23, had been out of work for several months. On this day his hopes were high because he was on his way to apply for a job which seemed just right for him. As Charlie rode the elevator to his interview, a stranger said pleasantly, 'Nice day, isn't it?' Just then Charlie happened to see his reflection in a mirror by the elevator buttons. His hair was sticking up in a peculiar way and he had no comb with him. He turned to the friendly stranger and asked, 'Do you have a comb I could borrow for a minute, please?'

Would this be an appropriate comment and what would be the effect on the stranger?

> Keith, age 25, was a clerk who worked in an office in the city. At noon, he took his lunch to a small park and sat on a sunny bench to eat. Often he tore part of a sandwich into bits, scattering it on the ground for pigeons. One day when he came to his favourite bench a pram was parked beside it. Keith noticed that a young woman was pushing an older child on a nearby swing. The baby in the pram began to cry but the mother did not hear this because the swing was squeaking. Now, Keith had learnt that when his baby nephew screamed, sometimes this meant that a pin in his nappy had opened. Rather than bother the mother in the park, Keith quickly checked the baby's clothing to see whether he could feel an open pin.

Do you think he should have checked the baby's clothing, and what could the woman think was happening if she saw Keith? What else could he have done?

○ Social reasoning skills can be illustrated by using scenes from the American television comedy programme *Third Rock from the Sun*. A group of aliens takes on human form. Comedy is created when they attempt to socialise like other humans. Their confusion and errors have some similarities to those experienced by adolescents with Asperger's Syndrome.

○ The poetry and autobiographies of people with Asperger's Syndrome describe how others have experienced the same situations and feelings. This provides an opportunity to explore the concept of empathy. There is a range of autobiographies in print, and these have recently been reviewed by Francesca Happé (1991). The group can also compose their own poetry or life stories. The following are examples from a social skills group:

> One foot in and one foot out
>   is what Asperger's is all about.
> Sometimes I think why me;
>   other times I think it's the best way to be.
> A little different from the rest
>   makes you think you're second best.
> Nobody quite understanding
>   a hard life which is very demanding.
> I look like any other child
>   but little things just make me wild.
>
>   (Vanessa Royal)

The group leaders can collect examples from other individuals with Asperger's Syndrome, such as the following poems:

> People everywhere,
>   Talking, wearing bright colours.
>   The talking is like the pounding of horses' hooves.
>   The bright colours are blinding,
>   The talking hurts my ears,
>   The bright colours hurt the eyes.
>   Oh why can't people be quiet and wear dull colours.
>
>   (Dianne Mear 1994)

> Humans are the most illogical race.
> Nothing they say,
> Nothing they do,
> Makes any sense.
> Oh, why can't humans be logical?
>
>   (Dianne Mear 1994)

A common theme is of building bridges, as described in this poem by Jim.

> I built a bridge
> out of nowhere, across nothingness
> and wondered if there would be something
> on the other side.
> I built a bridge
> out of fog, across darkness
> and hoped that there would be light on the
> other side.
> I built a bridge
> out of despair, across oblivion
> and knew that there would be hope on the
> other side.
> I built a bridge
> out of hell, across chaos
> and trusted that there would be strength on
> the other side.
> I built a bridge
> out of hell, across terror
> and it was a good bridge, a strong bridge,
> a beautiful bridge.
> It was a bridge I built myself,
> with only my hands for tools, my obstinacy
> for supports,
> my faith for spans, and my blood for rivets.
> I built a bridge, and crossed it,
> but there was no one there to meet me on
> the other side.

(Cesaroni and Garber 1991, p.311)

○ Sometimes it is necessary to explain that the situation where the person was unsure of their social competence was not necessarily their fault. The following is an illustration from the diary entry of a participant in a social skills group:

> Tonight is a social skills night. We had a very good talk about reading people's body language. It is not easy to see what they are

thinking without knowing what they are thinking, like you know if someone is stressed but you don't know why they are. I assume it's me.

- Provide guidance on body language, with a translation of each posture. This can become a game of 'guess the message'.

- Rehearse what to do in prospective situations, for example when a person may be teased or bullied or want to ask another person for a dance or date.

- A video camera and recorder can enable participants to view their performance. It is helpful to ensure the comments are predominantly positive. Presentation and comments can take on the format of a television game or talent show, but it is important not to let the participants be distracted by the technology.

- Once the participants have acquired skills that are proficiently demonstrated within the group, there may still be a problem of initiation and generalisation. That is, the person knows what to do but cannot make the first move or does not recognise the cues that indicate that the skills can be used in different situations. It is important to have practical exercises and monitoring that occurs between sessions. Parents and teachers must be informed of newly acquired skills to ensure they are practised in different circumstances. One of the advantages of having ordinary children in the group is that they can prompt and support group members in natural settings when there is no teacher or parent present.

- Prepare a story or play where the qualities of the person with Asperger's Syndrome are an advantage. He is the hero. The qualities include an eye for detail, remembering scenes, honesty and encyclopaedic knowledge of his special interest.

- Examine the biographies of famous scientists and artists for indicators of whether they had the same attributes and personal experiences as members of the group. This could be a homework or library exercise. The biographies of Einstein or Mozart would make a good starting point.

- M. Ann Marquis has adapted the game of Trivial Pursuit to become a board game to teach social skills. The following are examples of the questions:

  - Which word beginning with 'i' means making a comment about someone that hurts the person's feelings?

  - What would you do if someone gave you a gift that you really didn't like?

  - Your friends are all planning to do something that you feel is wrong, what would you do?

Answers are provided but the questions can also promote group discussion and emphasise that in some situations there may be more than one option. Details of how to obtain this game and similar games are included in the Appendix.

- Role play situations where the person has to learn when not to state the obvious or speak their minds, as this may be considered embarrassing or offensive to the other person. There are times when it is better not to say anything.

- Activities where the participants have to describe key individuals in their life, using terms that describe not only their physical characteristics but also their personality and what they like/dislike about them.

- Social skills groups can also include activities to improve conversation skills and the understanding and expression of emotions. These activities will be outlined in a subsequent section of this book.

Social skills groups can be both educational and entertaining. The duration of each session or course will vary according to the ability levels and rate of progress of the participants. Eventually, we will develop and evaluate more effective activities. In the meantime, parents, teachers and therapists can combine their knowledge and imagination to design a unique course for each child's profile of abilities with social behaviour.

Friendship

Research has identified a sequence of developmental stages in the concept and expression of friendship. As children mature they also change their opinion on what constitutes friendly behaviour. Sue Roffey and colleagues have described the complex interactions between intellectual and moral development and social experiences, and outlined four stages (Roffey, Tarrant and Majors 1994).

During the pre-school years children gradually change from playing *alongside* someone to playing *with* them. They learn that some games and activities cannot happen unless there is an element of sharing and turn-taking. They also aquire alternative means of dealing with conflict, becoming less egocentric and possessive of equipment. The most popular children are those who make positive initiatives such as 'let's go and play with …', and clearly welcome the company of others and include them in their play. Their explanation of why someone is their friend is predominantly based on simple measures such as proximity. Sue Roffey uses the following quote from a three-year-old to illustrate this stage of development:

> 'Why is Julio your friend?'
>
> 'Because I like him."
>
> 'Why do you like him?'
>
> 'Because he's my friend.'
>
> 'Why else do you like him?'
>
> 'Because he lives next door.' (p.1)

Thus it is important that the young children with Asperger's Syndrome are encouraged to share, invite someone to join their activity, and make positive initiatives of what to do.

The next natural stage occurs between the ages of five and eight years. Children start to understand that there is an element of reciprocity needed to maintain the friendship. Friends also fulfil practical needs, are helpful and simple aspects of the other person's personality become important. A friend is someone you can rely on for assistance, or lends you items you need. Children who are regarded well

by their peers are those who make friendly or complimentary acts. Sue
Roffey uses the following quote from a six-year-old:

'Why is Martina your friend?'

'Because she sits next to me and lends me her pencil.'

'Why else is she your friend?'

'Because she comes to my party and I go to hers.' (p.1)

and quotes such as:

'A friend is someone who makes you feel happy.'

'A friend shares things with you.'

Children with Asperger's Syndrome who are at this stage of the
development of the concept of friendship need to learn to make
compliments about their prospective friend, to show caring and
concern and to help others in both practical matters and activities at
school such as peer tutoring.

The third stage is in the pre-adolescent period from nine to thirteen
years. Around this age there is a clear gender split and friendship is
based on similarity, shared exploration, emotional support and an
increasing awareness of how they might be viewed by others. Friends
can be inseparable with shared intimacies. For example, a nine-year-old
was asked:

'Why is Peter your friend?'

'Because we have a laugh together.'

'Are there any other reasons?'

'He helps me when I can't spell something.'

A friend is 'someone you can talk to and who listens to you.'

A friend 'should be kind to you and not bully you.' (p.1)

As friendship at this stage can be based on shared interests, it is
important that children and adolescents with Asperger's Syndrome
have the opportunity to meet people who have the same abilities and
interests, learn the importance of self disclosure and listening as well as
to recognise the thoughts and feelings of others. Unfortunately they

can have some difficulty 'breaking into' established friendships and can be devastated when a genuine friendship has to end.

The fourth stage occurs during adolescence where friendship is based on trust, higher levels of self disclosure and greater emphasis on mutual or admired aspects of personality. There is also a movement from friendship pairs to groups with shared values. A thirteen-year-old was asked:

> 'Why is Amber your friend?'
>
> 'Because I can trust her with my secrets.'
>
> 'Why else is she your friend?'
>
> 'Because we think the same way about things.' (p.1)

The adolescent with Asperger's Syndrome can have difficulty with intimate self-disclosure, as they prefer their friendships to be platonic. They usually need advice on the changing needs and demands of friendships and need to identify with their own heroes and small circle of potential friends. They can be relatively more relaxed and socially fluent with just one friend, but as with the saying 'two's company and three's a crowd', they can become withdrawn and solitary when in a group. Their value systems are also likely to be more similar to adults than to adolescents and this can form a barrier to friendships with their peers. However, it is not impossible for adolescents with Asperger's Syndrome to find and maintain friendships that can last a lifetime. What they require is opportunity and support.

In early years, the child with Asperger's Syndrome may be unconcerned as to their lack of friends, and when asked to define friendship may provide immature descriptions (Botroff *et al.* 1995). Young adults may also be unsure of what constitutes a good friend. One person replied, 'someone who carries things for you, or lends you money', but could not think of anything other than practical attributes. The child may be asked if they have friends at school and home and reply that they do. However, conversation with parents and teachers and observation of the child indicates that this is wishful thinking or that the child is unaware that they are more a casual acquaintance than a true friend.

There is a range of school projects, books and activities that encourage children to explore the concept of what makes a good friend, and these are an essential part of the curriculum for children with Asperger's Syndrome. It is also important to identify natural instances of friendship, with the comment, 'that was a friendly thing to do' – or ask the child, 'what should a friend do in such circumstances'. Teachers can make worksheets based on the qualities of friendship. A book by Rozanne Lanczak (1987) provides relevant activities for children of primary school age. For example, a worksheet could use the following:

- Everyone likes .... and wants to be her friend because she is: ....

- Write about the ways .... helps her friends:

- Draw a picture of yourself being friendly and helpful. Write about it.

- Your best friend is in the hospital. What can you do and say to cheer up your friend?

- How do you feel when you're with your best friend?

- What do you like to do for your friends?

There are also group activities such as a circle of children discussing how can you tell if someone likes you, what do friends do or what could you do or make for your friend.

Sometimes the child can be attracted to, and attempt to make friends with, the most conspicuous children in their class. These may not be the most appropriate children to be friends with. The interest may be mutual, however, and the child may be criticised for imitating their behaviour. One may have to discourage some friendships and encourage others.

There is also the problem of other children taking advantage of their naivety. They can enjoy 'setting them up' and getting them in trouble. One teenage girl at an austere Catholic boarding school was asked by her 'friends' to go up to the teacher, who was a nun, and ask her a particular question. This she did, unaware of the obscene nature of her request. She was subsequently expelled. It is important that teachers are aware that there may be no mischievous intent and ask the child, 'Did anyone tell you to do this?' before considering punishment.

In the teenage years the person may become acutely aware of a lack of genuine friendship and exclusion from the social activities of their peers. They may become depressed or completely deny there is anything wrong with themselves, developing a sensitivity to the merest suggestion of being different. There can be confusion and despair as to why others are always the centre of attention and have an abundance of friends. When the person with Asperger's Syndrome tries the same activities or tells the same jokes, they are ridiculed. In such circumstances the person reluctantly has to agree they are different and need help before they will consider advice and a social skills group to improve their ability to make and maintain friendships.

Preference for solitude or odd attempts at socialising can be misconstrued by other teenagers. When the person is not interested in romantic relationships, they can be marginalised and attributed with being gay. These comments can be very painful for the confused adolescent with Asperger's Syndrome. Another teenager would be able to discuss these criticisms and their personality and sexuality with their best friend, but sadly, they may have no such person. However, parents or siblings can become substitute best friends and encourage self-disclosure about the emotional trials and tribulations of the day. This probably won't be when they have just returned from school, but later in the evening when they are relaxed and ready to talk and listen. The role here is of being a best friend who is offering support and consolation and encouraging self-esteem.

There are popular books on making friends written for ordinary teenagers that can be extremely relevant to the adolescent with Asperger's Syndrome. One such book by Andrew Matthews (1990) is written for the more able teenager. The text and cartoons outline some of the components and issues relevant to friendship, such as the value of listening, giving compliments, how to tell people they are wrong and admitting you are wrong. Experience has shown that the last two are particularly difficult for young adults with this syndrome.

There can be unusual ways of assessing whether a person may be a prospective friend. For example, one young man would judge a person's merits by asking very early in a conversation whether they drove their car with the sun visor up or down. If the person drove with it up, then the conversation ended abruptly. There can be a very 'black and white' approach to who could be a friend. The person may attempt to understand the concept of friendship by avidly watching TV soaps for models of actions and phrases. These programmes tend to overdramatise relationships and should not be the primary source of information on friendship. Sometimes the person with Asperger's Syndrome can misjudge the level of self-disclosure and embarrass a prospective friend or social group by revealing too much. Another concern is an assumption made by the person with Asperger's Syndrome that if they like someone, then the other person has the same degree of commitment. They may not recognise the other person's signals of a casual or platonic friendship.

There may eventually be a romantic interest for a particular person that is reciprocal and a relationship may develop. One young man was clearly upset when the typically brief early adolescent romance ended, stating 'life was easier when I didn't care' – a lament of many teenagers. Although he was delighted when he found a new girlfriend, he was also very confused when she didn't like the same things as his previous girlfriend. He had assumed that once he had learnt what to do and say, it could be duplicated for all subsequent girlfriends. However, this may not be a characteristic exclusive to Asperger's Syndrome.

Elizabeth Newsom (1985) and colleagues have explored the long-term development of children with Asperger's Syndrome by interviewing parents and individuals. The teenager's desire to have friends can be overwhelming, as described in the following quotation from a mother:

> He went to our local youth club – they were first of all thrilled, because Donald is tall, he makes a nice goalie, and all these little boys hero-worshipped him. But they soon found out – it doesn't take them an evening, you know, to find that something somewhere isn't OK. And he'd come back from the club, the first one – he must have tried about ten clubs all around here – he'd come back beaten up, spat at, his jumpers all torn … I said to him one day, 'Donald, why do you allow this? You are stronger than those boys, why do you let them?' And he said, 'Well, it's better than nothing, I don't mind.' And I think he was so desperate for some contact that to be beaten up was better than being alone.

And that was a nightmare, and that went on for year after year, one club after another. (p.9)

Another young man in his twenties went to discos with his friends and watched them meeting girls. He was aware of their flirtatious glances and body language and how the girls responded with a similar body language. But he could not imitate their body language and said, 'Girls' eyes go cold when they look at me. They give me these glances which say "Not for you, not for you". Despite his high academic achievement, he became depressed and self-loathing over his lack of a girlfriend.

In the search for popularity, the person may notice others who are competent in social discourse and attempt to mimic their personality, clothes and voice. It is almost as if they take on the persona of someone more successful than themselves (Williams 1992, 1994). This characteristic can be developed into a career as an actor. The person may also not follow the traditional codes of seeking friends of the same age range or social or cultural group. Unfortunately this may be misinterpreted by others.

Specific strategies can be learnt to maintain friendships. The person may have to memorise or write down key facts about each friend, such that when they see them or talk to them on the telephone they have a ready script of topics of conversation, with questions such as 'How is …?' One young woman tried always to remember that when there was a lull in the conversation with a particular friend, she should ask her about her home in London. However, this question became so automatic she often failed to remember that her friend had moved from London several years ago.

Some individuals have difficulty with the complex issues of morality and seek a blueprint of social conduct and behaviour in strong religious or political beliefs. This can also be an opportunity to meet people with similar characteristics and be certain of what is morally or socially appropriate. However, they may still have problems with the context. One young man considered the local group of Hells Angels (who were all of one ethnic minority group) as thieves and drug dealers from articles in the newspaper and told them this whenever he met them. Fortunately, he led a charmed life.

One way of making friends is to join clubs or associations based on the person's special interest. Computer clubs, historical societies, amateur astronomers or train spotters' meetings can provide a forum to learn about the interest and develop genuine friendships. The Internet, pen pals, and newsletters for people with Asperger's Syndrome have also provided opportunities to correspond, receive empathy and advice, and make friends. Contact addresses can be obtained from the local association for children with autism or Asperger's Syndrome and newsletters of national organisations.

The self-doubt and isolation of adolescence usually recede as the person matures. In secondary school one is in forced proximity with other teenagers, who are not the most tolerant companions. As an adult, the person with Asperger's Syndrome has greater choice in activities, companions and the pace of life. Time is also a great tutor, and eventually skills that seemed so elusive in childhood are acquired. It is important to explain to teenagers that there will be light at the end of the tunnel, adding that this is a figure of speech and it isn't a train hurtling towards them! Eventually they may well meet someone who does understand and genuinely wants to be their friend. This is what happened to Jim:

> I had a friend – not a parent driven by love and obligation to want to reach me, not a professional who made a career of studying my condition, but just someone who thought I was interesting enough to want to get to know better – a friend who, with no formal background in psychology or special education, figured out for herself some guidelines for relating to me. She told me what they were: never to assume without asking that I thought, felt, or understood *anything* merely because *she* would have such thoughts, feelings, or understanding in connection with my circumstances or behaviour; and never to assume without asking that I *didn't* think, feel, or understand anything merely because I was *not* acting the way she would act in connection with such thoughts, feelings, or understanding. In other words, she learned to *ask* instead of trying to *guess*. (Sinclair 1992, p.296)

As previously explained, psychological research has established that similarity is one of the main criteria for selecting friendships. This has led many people with Asperger's Syndrome to find friendships with other people who have the same diagnosis. Indeed some of these friendships have developed into a successful marriage.

Eye Contact

Clinical observation indicates that the child often fails to use eye contact to punctuate key parts of the conversation, for example when starting their utterance, to acknowledge praise or interest, seek clarification, to read body language or to signify the end of the utterance. Recent research studies (Baron-Cohen *et al.* 1995; Tantam, Holmes and Cordess 1993) have also suggested there is a lack of eye gaze when the other person is talking. Several adults with Asperger's Syndrome have described how it is easier to make eye contact when they don't have to listen. Eye contact breaks their concentration. There is also a failure to comprehend that the eyes convey information on a person's mental state or feelings. During a diagnostic assessment, a teenager with Asperger's Syndrome became anxious when talking about his special interests, as his parents had told him not to; they felt it made him appear odd. However, from a diagnostic point of view, there are qualitative aspects about the interests that are relevant. His means of coping with his anxiety was to close his eyes. When the comment was made to him that it was difficult to maintain a conversation with someone whose eyes were closed, he replied, 'Why would I want to look at you when I know where you are?' Clearly, the child with Asperger's Syndrome needs to learn the importance of looking at the face and eyes of the other person, not just to locate them but to recognise and respond to the subtle cues given in facial expressions.

Lorna Wing (1992) has referred to a person with Asperger's Syndrome who said 'people give each other messages with their eyes, but I do not know what they are saying'. Eye gaze and looking at people's faces can be extremely difficult for the person with Asperger's Syndrome as described in the following quotation:

> Looking at people's faces, particularly into their eyes, is one of the hardest things for me to do. When I do look at people I have nearly always had to make a conscious effort to do so and then I can usually only do it for a second. If I do look at people for longer periods of time, they usually claim that I seem to be just

looking through them rather than actually at them, as if I am unaware that they are actually there. People do not appreciate how unbearably difficult it is for me to look at a person. It disturbs my quietness and is terribly frightening – though the fear decreases with increasing distance away from the person. I have been trying to work on making eye contact whilst at hospital and whilst being treated by my consultant psychiatrist, but it has taken two-and-a-half years and has not been successful. My psychiatrist does not force me to look at him, although he insists on looking at me. He has explained that people might wrongly interpret my not looking at them as my being uninterested in them, that I am being untruthful about something or just rude. I am trying hard, because I do not want people thinking wrong things like this, but at the very best I can only look at somebody for a couple of seconds. It is almost as bad having other people looking at me as it is me looking at them. I have only just recently realised that when I look at people and pictures, I am not looking at the whole but rather just the outline of a part. I *can* look at a picture completely, but only a small section at a time. It is the same with people's faces. I cannot take in the whole face in one go. (Jolliffe *et al.* 1992, p.15)[1]

The person may eventually learn when and how to use eye contact, but some only learn to make this attribute less obvious. For example, Candy, a woman who has Asperger's Syndrome, described how as an adult 'eye to eye contact is now easier to maintain, but I look but do not see'.

Emotions

The original list of features for Asperger's Syndrome includes the comment that the child lacks empathy. This should not be misinter-

---

1   The person who wrote this description was originally diagnosed as having autism as a child and according to the diagnostic criteria of DSMIV, she does not have Asperger's Syndrome. Yet both conditions are considered as specific areas on the same continuum. Her descriptions of the personal experience of autism are invaluable in assisting our understanding of Asperger's Syndrome. This is illustrated by the quotations from her personal account of autism that are used at several points in this book.

preted as meaning that the child completely lacks the ability to care for others. It is more that they can be confused by the emotions of others or have difficulty expressing their own feelings. Although the child with Asperger's Syndrome usually has a natural symmetry of facial features, during conversation or when playing with the young child one notices an almost wooden quality. The child does not display the anticipated range and depth of facial expression. This can also occur with body language. Hands may be moved to describe graphically what to do with objects or express anger or frustration, but gestures or body language based on an appreciation of another person's thoughts and feelings – e.g. embarrassment, consolation or pride – are conspicuously diminished or absent (Attwood *et al.* 1988; Capps *et al.* 1992). As interaction continues, one is aware that the child is not recognising or responding to changes in the other person's facial expression or body language. Other children know how crossed arms indicate that the other person has come to the end of their tether, or a glint in the eye and certain tone of voice means 'I'm teasing you'. Unfortunately, subtle cues may not be recognised by the child with Asperger's Syndrome. For example, a mother was very annoyed with her young son and her deep frown was consistent with her mood. He then pointed to the folds of skin between her eyebrows and said, 'Eleven'. He was intrigued by the new pattern and oblivious to this clear signal of anger. The child can then be confused and offended when criticised for not complying with the signals or hidden intention. Parents report that they have to be overly dramatic in their body language, tone of voice and facial expression before the child recognises the other person's feelings.

Not only are there problems with the understanding of the emotional expressions of others, but the child's own expressions of emotions are unusual, and tend to lack subtlety and precision. A complete stranger may be given a kiss on the lips, or distress is expressed quite out of proportion to the situation. Conversation may include appropriate advanced technical terms but events are described in terms of actions, not feelings. One of the activities used by the author in the diagnostic assessment of young children is to ask the child to label the emotion portrayed in photographs of children or to express in their own face a range of simple emotions such as happy, sad, angry, frightened or surprised. Some children use their hands to manipulate their mouth to produce a smile or make unusual facial contortions that bear little resemblance to the anticipated facial expression. This activity is very easy for other children, but the child with Asperger's Syndrome has considerable difficulty and tends to rationalise or intellectualise their difficulty. One child replied, 'How can I make a sad face when I feel happy?' Older children with Asperger's Syndrome can express simple feelings but have a particular difficulty with defining and expressing more complex emotions such as embarrassment and pride (Capps *et al.* 1992).

Strategies to Help Understand Emotions

People with Asperger's Syndrome find the 'land of emotions' to be uncharted territory. In the last few years there has been increasing interest in one of the most important components of social behaviour, namely the communication of emotions or feelings. The following quotation illustrates this confusion:

> On the other hand I tend not to like kisses, hugs and cuddles very much. If I do give anybody a hug and cuddle it has to be when I feel like it, not when they want it. The only person who gets a hug at the moment is my consultant psychiatrist. My GP says he is a very lucky man, but I do not understand what luck has to do with a hug. (Joliffe *et al*, 1992, p.15)

Remedial strategies involve teaching an ability that other children acquire naturally, so there is remarkably little resource material. The Appendix includes a list of books and games that the author recommends for children with Asperger's Syndrome, although a teacher or parent will inevitably have to make or collate some of their own material. The basic principle is to explore one emotion at a time as the theme for a project. For example, first explore the feeling 'happy', and provide as many illustrations as you can. There is the *Mr Men* series of books that includes *Mr Happy*, and songs such as 'If you're happy and you know it ...'. A project can be undertaken to find pictures for a scrap book or collage that illustrate happy faces as well as events that make people or the child happy. The child or class can list and grade all the words that describe the different levels of happiness. Older children can ask their classmates and adults what makes them happy, demonstrating individual preferences and differences. The concept can also extend to drawings, choice of colours, music, etc., that illustrate a particular emotion. Some of the key questions in the project are, 'What can you *do* to make someone feel happy?' and 'What can you *say* to make them feel happy?'

A useful strategy developed by the author is to take a page from the child's scrapbook that illustrates examples of being happy. Once these have been described, a life-size photograph of someone smiling is placed next to the page. This is explained as someone feeling happy. The next stage is to place a mirror adjacent to the photograph and ask the child to look at the illustrations, the smiling face and to use the mirror to make their own face look happy. The child has an opportunity to concentrate on relevant thoughts, observe a model of facial expression and to practise their own facial expression. This strategy of using a scrapbook, photograph and mirror can be applied to a range of feelings.

There is also an excellent game called Mr Face, which comprises a blank face and a selection of different eyes, eyebrows and mouths that are attached to the face with Velcro. The child has to choose the components to portray a designated emotion – for example, finding a 'happy mouth' or 'happy eyes'. There is also a computer game (see Appendix) that allows the child to select facial components to complete a cartoon face with a variety of emotions.

Worksheets can be constructed based on the book by Rozanne Lanczak (1987) – for example, a drawing or photograph of someone opening their Christmas presents, where the child has to complete the following exercises:

- How does he feel about getting lots of presents?
- Draw pictures of his happy family with happy faces.

Another activity is for the teacher or parent to model a particular level of happiness in their body language, tone of voice, face, etc., and ask the child, 'How do I feel?' and 'Do I feel a little bit happy or very happy?' This activity explores the different levels of expression.

Once a particular emotion and the levels of expression are understood, the next stage is to use the same procedures for a contrasting emotion such as 'sad'. A game can then be devised using pictures, stories or role play where the child has to choose which emotion is portrayed, 'happy' or 'sad'. This game starts on the extremes of the continuum between the two emotions, for example, the joy of Grandmother arriving and the sadness when she leaves. With sadness, one can also ask 'How would you know when someone is sad?', followed by 'What could you do or say to help them feel better?' Here the child learns to read the cues and what to do when you recognise them. The 'sad' scrapbook can also be used to determine why the child may be sad, when there is a lack of verbal fluency to use speech to describe feelings.

Once this format is understood, other emotional states can be introduced, particularly anger, anxiety and frustration as well as more positive emotions, particularly love and affection, satisfaction, surprise, or complex emotions such as pride, jealousy or embarrassment. A workbook can be designed to explore the events and thoughts that elicit a particular emotion in the child, and alternative responses. For example:

What makes you feel ………?

What can you do when you feel ………?

I am angry because ……….

A game of Feeling Hats can be used as a group activity. An emotion is written on a card that is pinned to a hat. Each child chooses and puts on a hat with its associated emotions and shares times when they have had those feelings. Another game uses feeling masks with each participant acting the emotion portrayed on the mask, or the game Simon Says, adapted to include feelings. There is also a range of story books that illustrate specific emotions (see Appendix 1).

For teenagers, the social skills group can include a game using two piles of cards. Written on each card in one pile is a designated emotion, e.g., happy, proud or jealous, while each card in the alternative pile provides an action, for example washing the dishes or eating breakfast. The game involves taking a card from each pile and role playing the action according to the emotion, while the other participants try to guess the activity, feeling and the degree of expression. Traditional activities in speech and drama lessons can also be modified for adolescents with Asperger's Syndrome to illustrate how to identify the other person's feelings, using mime, listening to audiotapes and reading poetry.

Natural circumstances can also be used to learn the specific cues to identify feelings. A parent or teacher can take advantage of a situation to point out the signals – for example, the furrowed brow and wagging finger or a prolonged stare and silence that have a very specific meaning and require a particular response. This is very relevant in the classroom where the child can be oblivious to the subtle cues from the teacher that are so obvious to other children. When the child is confused or recognises they have made an error, a safety phrase can be taught such as 'I'm sorry, I'm not sure what you want me to do', 'I did not mean to upset you', or the simple 'I'm sorry'. This will help defuse the situation and convey courtesy or naivety rather than belligerence or indifference. The cues that identify certain feelings may also have to be learnt by adults. For example, when Temple Grandin became successful in her work, she wrote: 'I had to learn to be suspicious. I had to learn it cognitively. I couldn't *see* the jealous look on his face.' (1995, p.14)

An essential component of these programmes is to describe and explore the events and comments that produce a particular feeling, both within the child and other people. Instances can be recalled when the child experienced a particular emotion, and then it can be explained that other people have the same feelings. This is the start of acquiring empathy.

One of the unfortunate consequences of being less able to comprehend the feelings of others is to act as a 'scientist' and conduct psychological experiments to explore people's response to statements that draw out an extreme emotional response. A very small minority of adolescents with Asperger's Syndrome will deliberately make provocative statements that may be quite macabre and misinterpreted as potentially criminal in order to explore people's reactions. There can be great delight in causing a dramatic response and achieving the ability to control and manipulate people's emotions. The person appears callous, but in reality they are only trying to understand how to influence and predict the feelings of another person. Clearly such 'experiments' should be discouraged and replaced by tuition in the understanding and expression of emotion. This is not an easy task and can be a lifelong study. One young man with Asperger's Syndrome has a PhD in physics and is conducting research within a prestigious university research team. His diversion at home is to develop a mathematical formula to predict human emotional behaviour. If he achieves his ambition he may win the Nobel Prize, and cause the unemployment of thousands of psychologists.

Strategies to Help Express Emotions

Here, the difficulty seems to be achieving an accurate and precise way to express a particular feeling. This is illustrated by the example of a child with Asperger's Syndrome who was standing next to his mother. Both were watching his younger sister on a swing. She fell, and ran crying to her mother for comfort. As she approached, he turned to his mother and said, 'What face do I make?' Clearly he recognised the signals, but did not know how to express his concern. There can be occasions when the person simply lacks the precise spoken vocabulary to express accurately the subtleties of emotional expression. A moderate level of annoyance may be expressed by the use of expletives and bombastic body language, perhaps learnt by observing the vivid portrayal of other children or actors in television programmes. The expression is excessively dramatic but the message quite clear. Here the person must learn the range of more appropriate and accurate phrases and actions. A useful visual activity is to draw a gauge or barometer that 'measures' the degree of a specific emotion. The points on that measure can be given numerical values and appropriate words and actions. The following is an illustration of a gauge for anger:

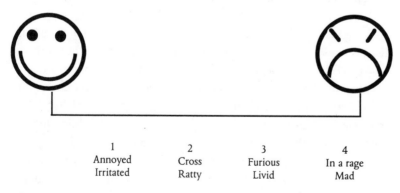

1	2	3	4
Annoyed	Cross	Furious	In a rage
Irritated	Ratty	Livid	Mad

Figure 2.1

For each point on the gauge the appropriate words, tone of voice and body language can be explained with illustrations from stories, television and role play. A game can be arranged where the teacher, parent or child demonstrates a particular feeling by action and appropriate words and the child has to point to the corresponding level of expression on the gauge. The child or adolescent can then be encouraged to use the gauge to express more precise and subtle words and body language. The gauge technique can be used for a range of emotions, but it has also proved very useful to encourage the expression of the degree of pain and discomfort. Children with Asperger's Syndrome are often very stoic, enduring pain with little evidence in their body language and speech that they may actually be experiencing agony.

Another activity is to make a workbook to explore the appropriate emotional and linguistic response to specific situations, for example, how would you feel and what can you say or do if:

- someone makes fun of your clothes
- someone criticises your handwriting
- you study hard for a test and get low marks
- you smile and say hello, but the other person ignores you
- you forget your lunch but a friend offers to share his lunch with you
- a friend says you know so much about computers.

The child can draw faces and scenes as well as write the script for each of these situations.

A confusing feature of Asperger's Syndrome is that sometimes mild distress is expressed as giggling, as in the saying 'you either laugh or you cry'. Here the child does not have a perverted sense of humour, just an expressive system that lacks subtlety and precision. It is important to explain the effect of such behaviour on other people, especially parents or teachers who may be criticising or punishing the child, and are annoyed that the child's reaction is to laugh. Occasionally the inappropriate laughter appears quite bizarre, perhaps upon hearing a certain word or phrase that produces almost hysterical laughter. Giggling can occur for no apparent reason and the person may be considered as experiencing auditory hallucinations. However, the reason can be quite simple and logical once you understand Asperger's Syndrome. The child often has a fascination with the meanings or sounds of words and an ambiguous phrase is intriguing, causing genuine humour, as occurs with puns. One adolescent was considered odd because he giggled to himself when alone in the school ground. The explanation was discovered when another child was asked why he didn't approach him and he replied, 'because he giggles at wasps'. Indeed, observation proved that his reaction to this venomous insect was to giggle, his means of expressing mild agitation. However, he had not considered that this behaviour would be of concern to other people and that they would think he was weird.

The expressive body language of the person with Asperger's Syndrome can be misinterpreted in other ways. Their manner can be misperceived as aggressive, aloof or indifferent and this can be a source of anxiety, especially for adults with Asperger's Syndrome. Shop assistants may think they are being quarrelsome or authoritarian, though that was not their intention. Here, role play and the use of video recordings can clarify which signals are being misinterpreted and enable practice of more subtle and precise speech and body language.

A common feature of Asperger's Syndrome is a difficulty with self-disclosure, that is, talking about one's inner feelings. The child may clearly be upset but does not have the ability or words to explain their feelings. A parent is left frustrated that they do not know why the child has such obvious anguish, and is therefore unable to provide appropriate sympathy and guidance. It will help if parents regularly model self-disclosure, that is, tell the person of their emotional reactions and thoughts during the day, and then use leading questions such as 'Did you feel angry at school today?', or 'Did you feel disappointed?'. This will provide an appropriate context and vocabulary to prompt self-disclosure.

Although there can be a problem with talking about one's feelings, there is often an eloquence that is quite remarkable in written or typed form, such as a diary, letter, poetry or autobiography. Candy, who has Asperger's Syndrome, described how 'the written language comes with ease and smoothness that is not available to be expressed any other way'. Try to encourage a diary, not solely of events, but also personal impressions, thoughts and feelings. A pictorial dictionary of feelings can be used with more able children, and the Appendix includes an example of a series of faces depicting emotions that act as prompts to find the appropriate word. This dictionary and the use of a diary proved extremely valuable for Fiona, an adolescent with Asperger's Syndrome. In class one afternoon, her teacher asked her to comply with a simple request. She could not complete the request and quickly became extremely agitated, knocking over furniture and eventually having to be excluded from the classroom. She offered no explanation and her teacher and mother were deeply concerned. That evening, in her diary, she described the following events and drew the appropriate faces to express her feelings at the time. During lunch, two senior girls had taken her lunch box, and as she tried to retrieve it they threw the box to each other in order to prevent her recovering it. This teasing was probably quite amusing to them, but extremely distressing for her, especially as she was subsequently unable to eat her lunch. When she returned to the classroom her body language and facial expression did not convey her inner agitation so her teacher was unaware of her level of distress, and approached her in the usual way. Hence the teacher's bewilderment as to why her response should be so dramatic and destructive.

Once the events that caused the behaviour were known, the failure to comply with the teacher's request was recognised as the 'trigger' to release the seething agitation. Two consequences followed – the girls were made to apologise to her, and she was encouraged to tell the teacher when she felt extremely angry or frustrated. The term 'a problem shared is a problem halved' is most appropriate here, but it may have to be explained to the person with Asperger's Syndrome that it applies to emotions as well as school work.

Finally, although learning social and emotional skills seems such an arduous task, it is surprising how well children with Asperger's Syndrome respond to their special programmes. The more intelligent and motivated the child and the greater the access to expertise and resources, the more rapid the progress. In due course we will know much more about why the errors occur and specific strategies to overcome these. Although we have only just started our journey down this particular road, we know it will lead to success.

Brief Summary of Strategies for Social Behaviour

- Learn how to:
  - start, maintain and end social play
  - be flexible, cooperative and share
  - maintain solitude without offending others
- Explain what the child should have done
- Encourage a friend to play with the child at home
- Enrol the child in clubs and societies
- Teach the child to observe other children to indicate what to do
- Encourage cooperative and competitive games
- Model how to relate to the child
- Explain alternative means of seeking assistance
- Encourage prospective friendships
- Provide enjoyment at break times
- Be aware of two characters
- Obtain teacher aide time
- Use Social Stories to understand the cues and actions for specific social situations
- Run social skills groups for adolescents to:
  - rehearse more appropriate options
  - demonstrate inappropriate social behaviour
  - use poetry and autobiographies to encourage self-disclosure and empathy
  - provide guidance and practice in body language

- ○ Projects and activities illustrating the qualities of a good friend
- ○ To help understand emotions:
  - explore one emotion at a time as a project
  - teach how to read and respond to the cues that indicate different levels of emotion
  - learn safety phrases when confused
- ○ To help express emotions:
  - use a 'gauge' as a visual guide
  - use video recording and role play to provide more subtle
  - or precise expression
  - use leading questions or a diary to encourage self-disclosure

CHAPTER 3

Language

Research suggests almost 50 per cent of children with Asperger's Syndrome are late in their development of speech, but they are usually talking fluently by the age of five (Eisenmajer *et al.* 1996). However, they appear distinctly odd in their being conspicuously less able to have a natural conversation. Although the acquisition of phonology and syntax (the pronunciation and grammar) follows the same pattern as other children, the differences are primarily in specific areas of pragmatics (i.e. how language is used in a social context); semantics (i.e. not recognising there may be several meanings); and prosody (i.e. an unusual pitch, stress or rhythm). Hans Asperger originally described the distinct profile of linguistic skills, and one of the diagnostic criteria of Carina and Christopher Gillberg (1989) is *unusual speech and language characteristics* with at least three of the following:

(a) delayed development

(b) superficially perfect expressive language

(c) formal pedantic language

(d) odd prosody, peculiar voice characteristics

(e) impairments in comprehension, including misinterpretations of literal/implied meanings.

Each of these characteristics will be explained in this chapter. Peter Szatmari and colleagues (1989) have the diagnostic criterion of odd speech, but add that the child may talk too much or too little, lack cohesion to the conversation and have an idiosyncratic use of words and repetitive patterns of speech.

The American Psychiatric Association and the World Health Organisation refer to language skills in their criteria, but state that 'there is no clinically significant general delay in language'. Unfortunately, this may be interpreted as an absence of any unusual qualities in language skills. By the age of five, the child with Asperger's Syndrome does not have a *general delay* in language, but does have problems with specific language skills. The most significant is in the area of pragmatics.

Pragmatics or the Art of Conversation

Here the problem is the use of language in a social context (Baltaxe *et al.* 1995; Baron-Cohen 1988; Eales 1993; Tantam *et al.* 1993). This is very evident when involved in conversation with someone with Asperger's Syndrome. During such conversations one becomes aware of several noticeable errors. The person may start the interaction with a comment irrelevant to the situation or by breaking the social or cultural codes. For example, the child may approach a stranger in the supermarket, their first utterance being, 'Do you have a cylinder mower?', and then proceed to give a monologue demonstrating encyclopaedic knowledge of garden machinery. Once the conversation has begun there seems to be no 'off switch' and only ends when the child's predetermined and practised 'script' is completed. Sometimes the parents can predict exactly what the child is going to say next. The child appears oblivious of their effect on the listener, even if the listener shows distinct signs of embarrassment or desire to end the interaction. One has the impression that the child is not listening to you, or does not know how to incorporate your comments, feelings or knowledge in their dialogue.

Thus, the young child requires tuition in the art of conversation. This includes conventional opening statements or comments and questions appropriate to the context. This can be learnt with role-play games where different circumstances are illustrated and an explanation given of why certain conversational 'openers' are inappropriate. Extreme examples can be demonstrated by the teacher, the child being asked to identify what was wrong and what the teacher should have said, with the child practising appropriate alternatives.

Other areas where the child may have difficulty are:

- repairing a conversation
- coping with uncertainty or mistakes
- overcoming a tendency to make irrelevant comments
- knowing when not to interrupt.

When a conversation becomes confusing, perhaps because the other person is imprecise or the anticipated reply is unclear, the natural reaction is to seek clarification. This ensures both people continue on the same 'track' or topic. When in doubt as to what to say, the person with Asperger's Syndrome has a tendency to have long pauses for thought before replying or to switch topics. Rather than saying, 'I'm not sure what you mean by that', or 'I'll have to think about that for a moment' the person with Asperger's Syndrome can take a considerable length of time to work out what to say in reply, or changes to a topic they are familiar with. This leads to a very ponderous conversation, or gives the impression that the dialogue always turns to the person's favourite interest. Although the initial topic may have been the summer vacation, within a few moments it has switched to dinosaurs.

There can be a reluctance to reply to a question when the person does not know the answer, and a lack of confidence to say 'I don't know' or 'I'm confused'. Here the child needs to learn how to explain their confusion and seek clarification. Appropriate phrases or replies have to be illustrated and taught, with the person not made to feel a failure if he or she is unsure what to say. One of the reasons that a specific interest has the potential to dominate conversations is that the person's considerable vocabulary and knowledge in this topic enhance fluency and comprehension. The person with Asperger's Syndrome also has a strong desire not to appear stupid. This is illustrated by a comment by Sean Barron:

> I had a driving need to ask questions about the states (of America) because I felt I could not talk the way 'normal' people talked, nor could I take part in their conversations, since I didn't understand them. Everyone else talked effortlessly, their conversations flowing as smoothly as a creek, and I felt very inferior, shut out, less important. I had to compensate for what

was lacking, and what better way than to show people that I knew all fifty states, their positions on the map, the shapes of each one? I needed to show everybody how smart I really was, and by asking the questions, I was doing just that. I never asked, 'What states have you been to?' but rather, 'Have you been to Montana?' so that I could show them I knew all the states. (Barron and Barron 1992, pp.107–108)

Another unusual feature is a tendency to make irrelevant comments. A statement or question can be made that is not obviously linked to the topic of conversation. These utterances can be word associations, fragments of the dialogue of previous conversations or quite bizarre utterances. It seems as if the child says the first thought that comes to mind, unaware how confusing this can be for the other person. The reason for this feature remains elusive. When this occurs, one is unsure whether to respond to the irrelevant comment or continue the conversation as if it had not occurred. The author tends to ignore such comments and focus on the central theme of the conversation.

There can also be a tendency to interrupt or talk over the speech of others. Temple Grandin (1995) describes how:

> During the last couple of years, I have become more aware of a kind of electricity that goes on between people. I have observed that when several people are together and having a good time, their speech and laughter follow a rhythm. They will all laugh together and then talk quietly until the next laughing cycle. I have always had a hard time fitting in with this rhythm, and I usually interrupt conversations without realising my mistake. The problem is that I can't follow the rhythm. (pp.91–92)

This section is entitled 'Pragmatics or the Art of Conversation', and Carol Gray (1994) has developed a technique entitled Comic Strip Conversations as a pictorial representation of the different levels of communication that occur in a conversation. Stick figures, speech and thought 'bubbles', symbols and colour are used to enable the child to see aspects they may not have been aware of.

For example, one of the potentially infuriating aspects of Asperger's Syndrome is a tendency to interrupt. The person has difficulty identifying the cues for when to start talking (i.e. a momentary pause, the end of the topic of conversation or the body language and eye contact that indicate 'your turn'). They may also not appreciate the effect of interrupting on the flow of conversation or the feelings of the other person. The skill of interrupting without causing offence or disruption is quite complex and difficult to explain, but a picture is worth a thousand words.

Carol uses the following Comic Strip Conversation to describe aspects of interruption:

Interrupt
when someone else is
not finished talking

Interrupt
when two people are
already talking

Figure 3.1 Interrupt: when my words bump into words from other people

This technique can be applied to a wide range of problems with conversation and social skills. The speech bubbles can be drawn in a variety of ways to convey emotion – for example, sharp edges to indicate anger or wavy lines to indicate anxiety. Colours can also be used. Happy or positive statements can be written in green while unpleasant thoughts could be written in red. A whole colour chart can be developed, for example embarrassed comments written with a pink marker, or sad feelings written in blue. These can then be translated into relevant aspects of the person's tone of voice or body language.

Comic Strip Conversations allow the child to analyse and understand the range of messages and meanings that are a natural part of conversation or play. Many children with Asperger's Syndrome are confused and upset by teasing or sarcasm. The speech and thought bubble as well as choice of colours can illustrate the hidden messages.

Carol has found that the children often assume that the other person is thinking exactly what they are thinking or they assume the other person was thinking exactly what they said and nothing else. The Comic Strip Conversations can then be used to show that each person may have very different thoughts and feelings in the same situation. Another advantage of this technique is that it can be used to represent the sequence of events in a conversation and illustrate the potential effects of a range of alternative comments or actions.

In a conversation we have cues that indicate a change of 'script'. For example, if during a conversation about a recent shopping expedition we learn that someone has had an unfortunate experience such as losing money, we tend to modify the script and offer sympathetic comments. The conversations of people with Asperger's Syndrome have fewer examples of spontaneous sympathetic comments. However, when an adult models an appropriate statement, children with Asperger's Syndrome can use this as a cue to provide their own sympathetic comments (Loveland and Tunali 1991). Thus, the significance of some cues may not be recognised, or the person requires some prompt or example to draw out a compassionate response. Should such a response be appropriate, a parent or teacher can make a compassionate comment first, which prompts the child to initiate their own appropriate comment. The child's curriculum also needs to include guidance using stories that illustrate the cues for comments of sympathy or a change of the script.

Other features of the art of conversation are to seek or comment on the opinions, abilities and experience of the other person, to offer sympathy, agreement and compliments, to make the topic interesting, and to know how and when to listen and look at the other person. These are remarkably complex and advanced skills that may be elusive for the child or teenager with Asperger's Syndrome. An activity for young children designed to encourage such skills is to organise a conversation between the child with Asperger's Syndrome and another child or adult, and have their teacher or parent next to them. The idea is to whisper in their ear what to say or do and when to say it. Their 'tutor' identifies the relevant cues and suggests or prompts appropriate replies, gradually encouraging the child to initiate their own dialogue and actions. An example is to whisper 'Ask Simon what is his favourite television programme', or 'Say I like that programme, too', so that the conversation is not restricted to a series of questions. A classroom activity to encourage conversation is to arrange the children to work in pairs. Each participant practises how to start a conversation with a stranger or maintain a conversation with a friend. The class will have previously identified the range of conversational openers such as 'How are you today?' or 'What do you think of the weather?' or a topical item on the news. They have also identified and remembered information about the other person and think of relevant questions or topics of conversation, for example, 'Did you enjoy your uncle's wedding?, 'Is your grandmother feeling better?' or 'What's your Dad's new car like?'. Another activity is to try to discover through conversation things they have in common. For adolescents, the curriculum for speech and drama classes can be modified to isolate, illustrate and practise the key elements of good conversation skills. Some children will need to learn the conversational script for particular situations, for example, when being teased, needing to be alone, asking for help or losing a game.

Before describing other unusual aspects of the language of people with Asperger's Syndrome, the following excerpt provides an opportunity for the reader to identify errors in the pragmatic aspects of language that occur during an encounter between Bill Bryson, the renowned author of travel books, and a person who appears to have Asperger's Syndrome. (1995)

> Over a long period of time it gradually dawned on me that the sort of person who will talk to you on a train is almost by definition the sort of person you don't want to talk to on a train, so these days I mostly keep to myself and rely for conversational entertainment on books by more loquacious types like Jan Morris and Paul Theroux. So there is a certain neat irony that as I

was sitting there minding my own business some guy in a rustling anorak came by, spied the book, and cried, 'Aha, that Thoreau chap!' I looked up to find him taking a perch on a seat opposite me. He looked to be in his early sixties, with a shock of white hair and festive, lushly overgrown eyebrows that rose in pinnacles, like the tips of whipped meringue. They looked as if somebody had been lifting him up by grabbing hold of them. 'Doesn't know his trains, you know,' he said.

'Sorry?' I answered warily.

'Thoreau.' He nodded at my book. 'Doesn't know his trains at all. Or if he does he keeps it to himself.' He laughed heartily at this and enjoyed it so much that he said it again and then sat with his hands on his knees and smiling as if trying to remember the last time he and I had had this much fun together.

I gave an economical nod of acknowledgement for his quip and returned my attention to my book in a gesture that I hoped he would correctly interpret as an invitation to **** ***. Instead, he reached across and pulled the book down with a crooked finger – an action I find deeply annoying at the best of times. 'Do you know that book of his – "Great Railway what's-it?" All across Asia. You know the one?'

I nodded.

'Do you know that in that book he goes from Lahore to Islamabad on the "Delhi Express" and never once mentions the make of engine.'

I could see that I was expected to comment, so I said, 'Oh?'

'Never mentioned it. Can you imagine that? What use is a railway book if you don't talk about the engines.'

'You like trains then?' I said and immediately wished I hadn't.

The next thing I knew the book was on my lap and I was listening to the world's most boring man. I didn't actually much listen to what he said. I found myself rivetted by his soaring eyebrows and by the discovery that he had an equally rich crop of nose hairs. He seemed to have bathed them in Miracle-Gro. He wasn't just a train spotter, but a train-talker, a far more dangerous condition.

'Now this train,' he was saying, 'is a Metro-Cammel self-sealed unit built at the Swindon works, at a guess I'd say between July 1986 and August, or at the very latest September, of '88. At first I thought it couldn't be a Swindon 86–88 because of the cross-stitching on the seatbacks, but then I noticed the dimpled rivets on the side panels, and I thought to myself, I thought, What we have here, Cyril my old son, is a hybrid. There aren't many certainties in this world but Metro-Cammel dimpled rivets never lie. So where's your home?'

It took me a moment to realise that I had been asked a question. 'Uh, Skipton,' I said, only half lying.

'You'll have Crosse & Blackwell cross-cambers up there,' he said or something similarly meaningless to me. 'Now me, I live in Upton-on-Severn – '

'The Severn bore,' I said reflexively, but he missed my meaning.

'That's right. Runs right past the house.' He looked at me with a hint of annoyance, as if I were trying to distract him from his principal thesis. Now down there we have Z-46 Zanussi spin cycles with Abbott & Costello horizontal thrusters. You can always tell a Z-46 because they go 'patoosh-patoosh' over seamed points rather than 'katoink-katoink'. It's a dead giveaway every time. I bet you didn't know that.'

I ended up feeling sorry for him. His wife had died two years before – suicide, I would guess – and he had devoted himself since then to travelling the rail lines of Britain, counting rivets, noting breastplate numbers, and doing whatever else it is these poor people do to pass the time until God takes them away to a merciful death. I had recently read a newspaper article in which it was reported that a speaker at the British Psychological Society had described train-spotting as a form of autism called Asperger's Syndrome.

He got off at Prestatyn – something to do with a Faggots & Gravy 12-ton blender tender that was rumoured to be coming through in the morning – and I waved to him from the window as the train pulled out, then luxuriated in the sudden peace. I listened to the train rushing over the tracks – it sound to me like it was saying 'asperger's syndrome, asperger's syndrome' – and passed the last forty minutes to Llandudno idly counting rivets. (pp.193–195)

Although Bill Bryson was annoyed, his companion probably thoroughly enjoyed the opportunity to give a monologue on his favourite interest.

Literal Interpretation

The person with Asperger's Syndrome tends to have a literal interpretation of what the other person says. For example, a young man was asked by his father to make a pot of tea. Sometime later his father was concerned that he had not received his refreshment and asked his son, 'Where's the tea?' His son replied, 'In the pot, of course.' His son was unaware that the original request implied the preparation and presentation of a cup of tea for each person. In a classroom, a teacher asked a child with Asperger's Syndrome to 'put your work right.' The child appeared confused, and slowly moved his workbook to the right of his desk. A father only just managed to stop his son complying with the request to 'go and ride your bike downstairs'. In the diagnostic and assessment clinic a girl was asked, 'Can you count to ten?' to which she replied 'Yes' and silently continued with her play. A friendly visitor to the family said to the child, 'You have your father's eyes.' This made the child extremely upset and he turned to his mother and said, 'I've got my own eyes, mom'. There can also be a literal interpretation of pictures. A child with Asperger's Syndrome was watching a 'Road Runner' cartoon, where the coyote fell from a cliff and suddenly produced an umbrella to substitute for a parachute. This was very confusing for the child who asked, 'Why would he do that if it wasn't raining?'

The person is not being deliberately annoying, or stupid. Rather, they are less aware of the hidden, implied or multiple meanings. This characteristic also affects the understanding of common phrases, idioms or metaphors such as:

Has the cat got your tongue?	Out of the blue.
Walk on ahead.	You're pulling my leg.
Keep your eye on the ball.	A flat battery.
Change your mind.	I caught his eye.
On all fours.	Over the moon.
Looks can kill.	Your voice is breaking.
Let's toast the bride.	Pull yourself together.

The author has observed that each of these has caused some confusion, and parents have to explain 'it's just a figure of speech'.

The previous chapter included a section on the Social Stories developed by Carol Gray. They can also be applied to help understand figures of speech, such as idioms. Carol used the following example of a Social Story to explain one of the above phrases:

> Sometimes a person says, 'I've changed my mind'.
>
> This means they had one idea, but now they have a new idea.
>
> I will work on staying calm when someone changes their mind.
>
> When someone says, 'I've changed my mind', I can think of someone writing something down, scratching it out and writing something new.

Children can nominate a phrase they have found confusing such as 'chill out' or 'catch you later', and guess the meaning of the statement. A story can be composed to explain their meaning and those situations when the phrases are used.

The person is often very confused by teasing. The rules of this game and the humorous intentions may not be recognised. Parents may have to explain they were only joking. For example, Robert was being asked about the events that caused him to bite the forearm of the Principal. The interviewer, with a tone of voice and body language that implied teasing or joking, asked whether he bit him because he was hungry. The child did not show any recognition of these cues, and calmly replied, 'No, I had eaten my lunch.' There is similar confusion when someone uses sarcasm, pretence or lies. When other children pretend to be a person from a popular television programme or film, the young child with Asperger's Syndrome is bewildered as to why they would change their name and character. There is also a problem with detecting when someone is lying.

Other children can obtain great enjoyment exploiting this naivete.

Making a literal interpretation can also lead to repeating problem-behaviour problems. For example, Donna Williams, in her autobiography, refers to how:

> The significance of what people said to me, when it sank in as more than just words, was always taken to apply only to that particular moment or situation. Thus, when I once received a serious lecture about writing graffiti on Parliament House during an excursion, I agreed that I'd never do this again and then, ten minutes later, was caught outside writing different graffiti on the school wall. To me, I was not ignoring what they said, nor was I trying to be funny: I had not done *exactly* the same thing as I had done before. (1995, p.61)

Parents, teachers and family members need to be aware of the child's propensity for a literal interpretation, and to stop and think how their comment or instruction could be misinterpreted or confusing The child can feel uncomfortable when the teacher starts to tell jokes, uses double meanings, sarcasm, irony or puns. Metaphors and some figures of speech will have to be explained. The child could have a school notebook to record examples and alternative meanings, and collect cartoons and draw scenes that depict literal interpretation. Carol Gray's Comic Strip Conversations is an ideal medium to explore these aspects of everyday speech. Whenever an error occurs, always explain the hidden intention or full meaning. This occurred with a teenage girl with Asperger's Syndrome who answered the telephone and was asked by the caller, 'Is Paul there?'. As Paul was not in the room, she replied, 'No', and promptly put the phone down. In this instance the caller, who was aware of her tendency to be literal, phoned again and explained that if Paul were not there, he would like her to find him and ask him to come to the telephone.

Prosody or the Melody of Speech

In conversation, we change vocal tone and volume to emphasise key words or indicate the associated emotion. When listening to the speech of a person with Asperger's Syndrome, one may be aware that there is a lack of variation in pitch, stress and rhythm, or the melody of speech (Fine *et al.* 1991). There can be a lack of modulation such that speech has a monotonous or flat quality, or an overprecise diction with stress on every syllable. Sometimes there are odd changes, as described by Donna Williams:

> I would often fluctuate between accents and pitch and the manner in which I described things. Sometimes my accent seemed quite 'polished' and refined. Sometimes I spoke as though I was born and bred in the gutter. Sometimes my pitch was normal, at other times it was deep like I was doing an Elvis impersonation. When I was excited, however, it sounded like Mickey Mouse after being run over by a steamroller – high-pitched and flat. (1995, pp. 74–75)

The child's accent may not be consistent with local children, perhaps maintaining the mother's accent (Baron-Cohen and Staunton 1994). One normally expects children's accents to change to that of their peer group at school. This is most noticeable when the family has moved to an area with a different accent. The child with Asperger's Syndrome is less likely to change their accent to that of other local children. Sometimes the child's accent is the same as occurs on their favourite television programmes. Parents may be asked why the child has an American accent (perhaps from watching Sesame Street), or people assume the child's family are recent immigrants from the United States. Once the child has heard a particular word or phrase, the original enunciation will be continued in such a way that the experienced listener may be able to identify whose accent is being echoed.

Should the child's tone be monotonous and thereby perceived as boring or odd (as with the voice of Mr Bean), then a speech therapist or speech and drama teacher may have to provide advice on how to improve the child's prosody, using the techniques developed by actors to change their accent, tone or emphasis.

The child may also have difficulty understanding the relevance of the change in tone, inflection or emphasis on certain words when listening to the speech of the other person. These subtle cues are extremely important in identifying the different meanings. The following example is taken from Andrew Matthews' book *Making Friends* (1990, p.129) and illustrates how the meaning changes when the emphasis is put on a different word:

I didn't say she stole my money.

I didn't say she stole my money [but *someone* said it].

I *didn't* say she stole my money [I *definitely* didn't say it].

I didn't *say* she stole my money [but I *implied it*].

I didn't say *she* stole my money [but *someone* stole it].

I didn't say she *stole* my money [but she did *something* with it].

I didn't say she stole *my* money [she stole *someone else's*].

I didn't say she stole my *money* [she took *something else*].

There are eight different meanings without changing one syllable. Role plays and speech and drama exercises can be used to explain how and why the emphasis changes. For example, Sue Roffey recommends the game,'Behind the Screen'. A child is given a list of adjectives or adverbs and asked to count from nought to ten out loud from behind the screen in the manner of the adjective or adverb. The rest of the group has to guess what the word might be. The alternative is a tone conversation. Working in pairs, one child starts a conversation or reads a script in a particular tone of voice, and their partner responds with the same tone of voice.

Pedantic Speech

During the person's adolescence, their speech may become pedantic or overly formal (Kerbeshian, Burd and Fisher 1990, Ghaziuddin and Gerstein 1996). For example, a teenager was helping his father in his job as an after-hours office cleaner and was asked to empty all the bins. A while later, the father was annoyed that several bins had obviously not been emptied. When he asked his son why, he replied, 'Those aren't bins, they're wicker baskets.' He was clearly being very pedantic, using a limited or literal interpretation of his father's request. However, this characteristic can be infuriating for both parties, as in the example of a young man in the United States who was fascinated by the potential maximum speed of different makes of vehicles and the speed limits in various countries. The conversation with a visitor from Australia progressed quite amiably until the visitor mentioned the value of low speed in conserving petrol. The young man suddenly became agitated, saying vehemently that the word is 'gasoline', not 'petrol'.

The choice of words can be overly formal, as in the example of a girl of five who, when she was collected from school by her older sister, asked her, 'Is my mother home?' The older sister's reply was, 'No, Mum's not home yet.' Clearly the family use the word 'Mum', but the girl with Asperger's Syndrome used an unusually formal way of referring to her mother. Children with this syndrome may address others by their full name – instead of saying, 'Hello, Mary', the child says 'Hello, Mary Smith'. Sometimes the choice of words would be more appropriate for an adult, and one has the impression of talking to an adult rather than a child. The choice of phrases and style has been learnt from adults, who may be a much more important influence in developing speech patterns than other children. Abstractions and a lack of precision are rarely tolerated, and one learns to avoid comments or replies using words such as maybe, perhaps, sometimes or later. For example, as the author of the following extract explains:

> Life is such a struggle; indecision over things that other people refer to as trivial results in an awful lot of inner distress. For instance, if somebody at home says, 'We may go shopping tomorrow', or if somebody says, 'We will see what happens', they do not seem to realise that the uncertainty causes a lot of inner distress, and that I constantly labour, in a cognitive sense, over what may or may not occur. The indecision over events extends to indecision over other things, such as where objects are to be put or found and over what people are expecting from me. (Jolliffe *et al.* 1992, p.16)

Sometimes the child will incessantly bombard the speaker with questions seeking reassurance about when the event will occur. To avoid ambiguity and be precise, the parents may become as pedantic as the child.

An Idiosyncratic Use of Words

The child appears to have the ability to invent unique words (or neologisms), or are idiosyncratic or original in their use of language (Tantam 1991; Volden and Loud 1991). A child with Asperger's Syndrome created the word 'snook' to describe a flake of chocolate in an ice block, and the word 'clink' for a magnet. Another child was asked why he was not interested in his baby brother and replied, 'He can't walk, he can't talk – he's broken.' When making his bedroom untidy, with toys strewn all over the floor, another child explained he was 'tidying down' (the opposite of tidying up). Yet another example is the girl who described her ankle as the 'wrist of my foot', and ice cubes as 'water bones'.

Sometimes the sound or meaning of a particular word provokes great laughter or giggling. The humour is idiosyncratic to the child but can be very puzzling to the teacher or parent. This ability to provide a novel perspective on language is fascinating, and one of the endearing and genuinely creative aspects of Asperger's Syndrome. Perhaps the child could be given a creativity prize for lateral thinking that produces a novel word, phrase or description, and incorporate their unusual words or phrases when writing a story book.

Vocalising Thoughts

A characteristic of all young children is to vocalise their thoughts as they play alone or with others. By the time they start school they have learnt to keep their thoughts to themselves. Eventually, talking to oneself is considered by some members of the public as a sign of madness. Children with Asperger's Syndrome may continue to vocalise their thoughts many years after one would expect their thoughts to be silent. This often disrupts the attention of other children in the class, or causes teasing when they talk to themselves while alone in the playground. The child may also fail to hear the instruction of the teacher because they were too engrossed in their personal conversation. There may be several reasons for this behaviour. First, the child may be less influenced by peers to be quiet, or less concerned at appearing different. The vocalisations may also have a constructive purpose or be reassuring. For example, one person described how 'talking to myself helps me figure out and practice how to express ideas well', while another said:

> You know I like the sound of my own voice because it keeps me from feeling lonely. I think there is also a little fear that if I don't talk a lot I may lose my voice. I didn't talk until I was almost five, you know. (Dewey 1991, p.204)

Another reason is the person rehearsing the probable conversations for the following day or repeating conversations to try to fully understand them.

It is important to find out why the person talks to themselves. It could simply be developmental delay, a means of organising their thoughts or providing comfort. Should this aspect of language become a problem, then encourage the child to whisper rather than speak, and to try to 'think it, don't say it' when near other people. It is noticable that some adults with Asperger's Syndrome continue to have a tendency to silently move their lips in synchrony with their thoughts.

Auditory Discrimination and Distortion

Several autobiographies of people with Asperger's Syndrome have included reference to problems with focusing on one person's voice when several people are talking, or a distorted perception of their speech. A child with Asperger's Syndrome was in an open-plan classroom that comprised two classes. The teacher of his class was reading out a maths test while the teacher in the other class was reading out a spelling test. When his teacher marked his test paper, she noted he had written the answers to both tests. Candy described how 'many voices make speech difficult to understand', and the child can be very confused when too many people are talking at the same time, especially if they are all talking about the same topic, as occurs in the background chatter in a classroom.

The distortion of speech is explained by Darren White (White and White 1987):

> I was sometimes able to hear a word or two at the start and understand it and then the next lot of words sort of merged into one another and I could not make head or tail of it. (p.224)

> I was often lazy at school because sometimes my ears distorted the teacher's instructions or my eyes blurred to stop me seeing the blackboard properly and the teachers would say 'On with your work, Darren.' (p.225)

Donna Williams (1992) describes how:

> Anything I took in had to be deciphered as though it had to pass through some sort of complicated checkpoint procedure. Sometimes people would have to repeat a particular sentence several times for me as I would hear it in bits and the way in which my mind had segmented their sentence into words left me with a strange and sometimes unintelligible message. It was a bit like when someone plays around with the volume switch on the TV. (p.61)

Temple Grandin (1991) also refers to how:

> Even now, I still have problems with tuning out. I will be listening to my favourite song on the radio and then notice that I missed half of it. My hearing shuts off unexpectedly. In college I had to constantly keep taking notes to prevent myself from tuning out. (p.61)

Should such problems become apparent, perhaps appearing as 'selective deafness', then it is important for a speech pathologist or audiologist to assess the child's skills with the processing of auditory information. It will also help to encourage the child to ask the person to repeat what they said, simplify it or put into other words, despite their reluctance to seek help or their fear of being considered stupid. Another approach is to ask the child to repeat aloud your instruction if you suspect your speech was perceived as unintelligible. For example, asking 'Can you tell me what you've got to do?'

It may also help to pause between each sentence to allow the person time to process what you have said and to use written instructions. The advantages of these techniques are explained by the author in the following quotation (Jolliffe et al, 1992):

It is hard to reproduce and understand words that are similar in sound, like ball and bull, fend and vend, beam and bean, mum and numb, chase and case, bad and bag. Although people pick me up on any mispronunciations, they do not seem to notice that when they speak there is in every sentence words that are hard to distinguish, although after a bit of effort I can often work out what these words are from the context of the sentence. But when somebody talks to me I have to really try and listen carefully, if I am going to stand any chance of working out what the words are. At school and during my first degree I was helped by the fact that I could read up topics in advance, things were also written down on the blackboard, the work tended to follow a logical progression and because new material was being put across to students, teachers would not talk too fast, rather they seemed to leave gaps of a second or two between each sentence which enabled me to guess more accurately what I had heard. When I read books the problem of deciphering what the words actually are does not exist because I can see immediately what they are meant to be. (p.14)

The author has known of several adults with Asperger's Syndrome who have asked people not to speak when they are considering what to say in reply to a question as this can disrupt their thought processes and further delay their reply. Thus, the person is more likely to understand if they only have to concentrate on one voice, there is a brief silence between each instruction or question, and they can also read the information.

Verbal Fluency

The child may talk too much or too little. Sometimes their genuine enthusiasm for their area of interest leads to garrulous speech, a never ending 'babbling brook' (another example of a potentially confusing figure of speech). The voluble enthusiasm can be quite endearing – if occasionally tedious. The child is keen to demonstrate their knowledge and verbal fluency, as well as to learn new information about their interest. This subject may dominate their conversation, but it is an expression of their emotional and intellectual fascination. They may have to learn the cues when to be quiet.

In contrast, some children may have periods when they are genuinely 'lost for words' or even mute. Clinical experience has identified children with Asperger's Syndrome who will only talk to other children and their parents and are electively mute with other adults. One child became mute as soon as he entered the school grounds. We are still unsure why this occurs, but a recent autobiography may provide an explanation (Jolliffe et al. 1992):

> Speaking for me is still often difficult and occasionally impossible, although this has become easier over the years. I sometimes know in my head what the words are but they do not always come out. Sometimes when they do come out they are incorrect, a fact that I am only sometimes aware of and which is often pointed out by other people.

> One of the most frustrating things about autism is that it is very difficult to explain how you are feeling; whether something hurts or frightens you or when you are feeling unwell and you cannot stick up for yourself. I take Beta Blockers sometimes to reduce the physical symptoms of fear and although I can now tell people if something frightens me, I can never actually tell them while the event is occurring. Similarly, on several occasions when I have been asked what my name is by a stranger I cannot always remember it and yet when I am more relaxed I can remember phone numbers and formulae after just hearing them once. When I am very frightened by somebody or something, or I am in pain, I can often make motor movements and a noise, but the words just do not come out. (p.14)

Thus, being lost for words or even mute may be due to a high level of anxiety. Certainly some adults with Asperger's Syndrome are prone to stuttering when anxious. Here the problem is not strictly an impairment in language skills, but the effect of emotion on the ability to speak. Should this problem become apparent, there is a range of strategies to help the person with Asperger's Syndrome cope with anxiety. These will be described in a subsequent chapter.

Brief Summary of Strategies for Language

Pragmatics

- Learn
  - appropriate opening comments
  - to seek clarification or assistance when confused
- Encourage confidence to admit 'I don't know'
- Teach the cues of when to reply, interrupt or change the topic
- Model sympathetic comments
- Whisper in the child's ear what to say to the other person
- Use speech and drama activities on the art of conversation
- Use Social Stories and Comic Strip Conversations as a verbal or pictorial representation of the different levels of communication

Literal Interpretation

- Think how your comment or instruction could be misinterpreted
- Explain metaphors and figures of speech

Prosody

- Teach how to modify stress, rhythm and pitch to emphasise key words and associated emotions

Pedantic Speech

- Avoid abstractions and lack of precision

Idiosyncratic Words

- A genuinely creative aspect of Asperger's Syndrome to be encouraged

Vocalising Thoughts

○ Encourage whispering and 'think it, don't say it' when near other people

Auditory Discrimination and Distortion

○ Encourage asking for the instruction to be repeated, simplified, put into other words or written down

○ Pause between instructions

Verbal Fluency

○ Anxiety may inhibit speech and require treatment.

CHAPTER 4

Interests and Routines

Two characteristics of Asperger's Syndrome that have not been adequately defined in the literature are the tendency to become fascinated by a special interest that dominates the person's time and conversation and the imposition of routines that must be completed. This is despite the clinical evidence that these characteristics have a significant influence on the sanity of the family and the research evidence that this feature is relatively stable over time (Piven *et al* 1996). The young child may develop an interest in collecting specific items, as described in the following autobiography (Jolliffe *et al.* 1992):

> I also liked collecting the lids of tubes of Smarties. These were orange, green, blue, red and yellow and had a letter of the alphabet on. I had more orange ones and only a few blue ones and I never got all the letters of the alphabet. The only problem was that I wanted to take the lids off all the tubes of Smarties when I was in a sweet shop so that I could see what the letter was underneath and this seemed to make other people angry. (p.13)

Some collections, such as the one described above, comprise items accumulated by other children or adults. Examples include the labels from bottles of beer, butterflies or key rings, while others are distinctly unusual, for example, yellow pencils, vacuum cleaners or toilet brushes. The accumulation of the latter item caused some distress for the child's family, as his first action upon entering a house was to collect and inspect the toilet brush. They subsequently discovered who were their true friends.

There is an intense interest in collecting these items at every opportunity. The child appears to have a visual acuity that identifies each specimen from some distance and cannot be distracted or persuaded to abandon an opportunity to collect just one more. Eventually the child decides to change to a new type of object but this continues to be a solitary pursuit and often independent of the latest craze of their peers. One child requested that all his presents at his birthday party should be road signs. With some ingenuity, his parents were able to ensure his request was granted.

There appears to be a developmental sequence in the nature of the interests, and the next stage is a fascination with a topic rather than an object. Common topics are transport (especially trains and trucks), dinosaurs, electronics and science. The person develops an encyclopaedic knowledge, avidly reading information about their interest, and asking incessant questions. However, the interest is primarily a solitary pursuit, and not the latest craze of their peers. A common feature is a fascination with statistics, order and symmetry. For example, one seven-year-old boy with Asperger's Syndrome became extremely keen on rugby league. He avidly watched matches on television, memorised the commentary, knew the scores of previous matches and the league positions of each team. He would literally talk for hours on this topic. His parents decided to make practical use of his interest by enrolling him in a junior team. As the whistle blew to start his first game, he immediately began a loud and continuous commentary on the action as if he were a sports commentator. When the ball was eventually passed to him, he threw it away in disgust. He was completely uninterested in actually playing the game.

Sometimes the interest can be quite ingenious. A young man was fascinated by trucks, and the different manufacturers and models. As he walked home from work, he would remember each truck he saw and assign the vehicle points based on its rarity. A Volvo truck was relatively common and would only achieve one point for its manufacturer, while a Mercedes truck was rare and would achieve five points. When he arrived home, he would distribute the points to adjust his unique league table of truck manufacturers.

The interest may be expressed in art with a fascination with perspective, detail or architecture. Electronics and computers are another interest that may be pursued, sometimes without respect for safety. One young man was intrigued by electronic circuit diagrams and camera flash units. This included a curiosity regarding how such a unit would tolerate being connected directly to the house electricity supply. He survived the explosion!

Young children can develop a passionate interest in pretending to be a person or animal. One seven-year-old girl became fascinated by the stories and lifestyle of Vikings, and persuaded her mother to make her a sheepskin tunic and pudding bowl with horns as a helmet. She then wandered around her local village in her costume telling everyone she was a Viking. Other examples are being an electrician, policeman and bricklayer. The interest involves considerable imagination and creativity with the child avidly learning about the lifestyle or trade. However, they are usually solitary pursuits that dominate their thoughts and play. They can be quite eccentric with the child continuously pretending to be an animal such as an ant, horse or even an alien. The interest is intense but brief, and leads to a change in the usual choice for the parents' reading material at bedtime. Eventually the bedroom and home are cluttered with material relevant to each interest that can never be thrown away.

Perhaps the final stage is a romantic rather than intellectual interest in a real person. This is more likely to occur during or after adolescence and may be similar to an adolescent 'crush' or infatuation. The individual who is the focus for adulation may be mystified as to their intentions and parents concerned how this may be misinterpreted. One teenage girl with Asperger's Syndrome became a devoted fan of a pop star. Her paintings and sculptures of him were remarkably skilled and attentive to detail to such a degree that her work was given prominence by a national newspaper. The pop star was impressed, a correspondence ensued and they eventually met. A genuine friendship developed and she frequently stayed at the home of her 'hero' and his wife. Yet one day she chose never to have any contact with him again. He had bought a dog and she could not tolerate the sound of barking. He was never mentioned again. However, within a few weeks, a new hero emerged.

The diagnostic criteria describe another characteristic that may be linked to or independent of the special interests. The young child with Asperger's Syndrome may have a propensity to establish and enforce routines. Parents have to comply as change or a lack of completion of the activity can lead to great distress and anxiety. Once a pattern has emerged it must be maintained. Unfortunately, the components of the anticipated sequence may increase over time. For example, the bedtime routine may have started with only lining up three toys, but becomes an elaborate ritual where dozens of toys have to be placed according to strict rules of order and symmetry. When a journey to a destination has followed the same route several times, there is the expectation that this must be the only route and no deviation is tolerated. The following quotation illustrates why there is a determination to create order (Jolliffe *et al*. 1992):

> Reality to an autistic person is a confusing, interacting mass of events, people, places, sounds and sights. There seem to be no clear boundaries, order or meaning to anything. A large part of my life is spent just trying to work out the pattern behind everything. Set routines, times, particular routes and rituals all help to get order into an unbearably chaotic life. (p.16)

Diagnostic Criteria Relevant to Interests and Routines

The Gillbergs' criteria (1989) for Asperger's Syndrome make clear reference to interests and routines. Their second criterion is the presence of *narrow interests*, with at least one of the following:

(a) exclusion of other activities

(b) repetitive adherence

(c) more rote than meaning.

Their third criterion refers to *repetitive routines*, with their imposition being either:

(a) on self in aspects of life

(b) on others.

Peter Szatmari and colleagues' criteria (1989) do not make reference to these two characteristics and clinical experience suggests that a small proportion of people with Asperger's Syndrome have a negligible expression of these features. Nevertheless, they are included in the criteria of the American Psychiatric Association and the World Health Organisation. At present there is considerable variation between the alternative diagnostic criteria in defining the nature of this characteristic, and some even doubt whether these should be diagnostic criteria. Nevertheless, should the person with Asperger's Syndrome have a special interest or routine that significantly affects their lives, then the following sections provide a tentative explanation of why they occur and what can be done to minimise their expression or find a constructive application.

Special Interests

The essential component of these interests is the accumulation of objects or information. Many people have a hobby, and having a special interest is not in itself significant. The difference between the normal range and the eccentricity observed in Asperger's Syndrome is that these pursuits are often solitary, idiosyncratic and dominate the person's time and conversation. They are also different from a compulsive disorder in that the person really enjoys their interest and does not try to resist it. So why do they occur? There are several explanations.

To facilitate conversation

If one is not a good conversationalist, perhaps unsure of the cues that indicate an appropriate topic or script and occasionally lost for words (especially if the topic requires social knowledge or empathy), then there is a comfortable assurance and fluency if the conversation is about a special interest. The words tumble out with ease from extensive knowledge and practice.

To indicate intelligence

A common aspiration for people with Asperger's Syndrome is not to appear stupid. One way to indicate intelligence is to deliver a monologue that includes technical terms unfamiliar to the listener. However, this characteristic is not exclusive to Asperger's Syndrome. Some computer experts, academics, lawyers and other specialists (including psychologists!) use exclusive terminology to imply superiority in knowledge. Indeed, some of these professions may provide the initial role model for this characteristic or become a career option.

To provide order and consistency

People with Asperger's Syndrome often have difficulty establishing and coping with the changing patterns and expectations in daily life. The interests tend to involve order, as in cataloguing information or creating tables. One of the reasons why computers are so appealing is not only that you do not have to talk to or socialise with them, but that they are logical, consistent and not prone to moods. Thus, they are an ideal interest for the person with Asperger's Syndrome.

A means of relaxation

These solitary and repetitive pursuits can be an opportunity to avoid the stresses associated with social contact and to relax in the security of routine. One lady had a special interest in conducting the Japanese tea ceremony several times a day. The ritual and symmetry would obviously be appealing, but when asked why she was so interested, she replied that it helped her to relax. It can certainly take one's mind away from the anxieties of the day. Clinical experience has indicated that the degree of interest is proportional to the degree of stress. The greater the stress, the more intense the interest.

An enjoyable activity

If socialising is hard work and not your first choice of something to do, and you are not interested in becoming a television 'couch potato', what else can you do to occupy your time? The interest is not only a means of occupying time. It also offers genuine pleasure. David Miedzianik (1986) describes how:

> It always fascinates me watching the gas man mending the stoves. It makes me very excited and I jump up and down when I see the gas flame burning. I've always jumped up and down since I've been a kid. (p.88)

A person with Asperger's Syndrome may have few pleasures in life. The indulgence in a special interest provides genuine enjoyment. The degree of excitement may make the person literally jump for joy.

How to Cope with the Special Interests

The problem for families is tolerating the incessant questions on the same topic, reluctance to consider any other activity, and access to the source material. Many parents ask how they can reduce or even eliminate a particular interest. This is not an easy task. The following are two suggestions:

Controlled access

Parents may have tried dissuading the child from continuing their interest by refusing access to the source material and offering encouragement to try something else. Experience has shown that the motivation to indulge in the interest usually exceeds any imposed motivation to stop.

A better approach is controlled access. The problem may not be the activity itself but its duration and dominance over other interests. Greater success has been achieved by limiting the time spent engaged in the activity using a clock or timer. When the timer goes off, the activity must cease. However, it is essential that the person is then encouraged to do some other activity that they enjoy and to ensure they cannot see the equipment relevant to the interest. In other words, 'out of sight, out of mind'. There must be something else to occupy the person's thoughts while the urge to continue the interest gradually subsides. Ask the person to complete a task with which they are familiar and successful in another room or go on some necessary errand. If the person is distressed then offer reassurance by referring to a timetable or schedule that clearly indicates when they can return to their interest. Basically, one is rationing access.

The interest may naturally last for several weeks or even decades, but when one interest ends, it will soon be replaced by another. If the interest is tolerable in small doses, then controlled access is appropriate. If the interest is unacceptable, i.e. illegal or could lead to dangerous activities (e.g. an interest in weapons, fires or poisons), then parents will need a programme designed by a clinical psychologist with experience with Asperger's Syndrome. The challenge here is to offer inducement not to indulge in the interest and to encourage an acceptable alternative. The first choice may be computers, as this interest is valued by other children, it is relatively easy to gain access to computer information and it can be a constructive occupation or career.

Constructive application

Children are motivated by the desire to please their teacher, parents or friends, to be competitive, cooperative, or to imitate the activities of other children. These desires are significantly reduced in the child with Asperger's Syndrome, and a common dilemma faced by parents and teachers is the child's lack of motivation for any activity they suggest. However the child has enormous motivation and attention when engaged in their special interest. The strategy here is to incorporate the interest in the activity that is non-motivating or perceived as boring. The child can also earn access to the interest by effort and compliance, and parents may consider how the interest could be used to encourage social contact or become a vocation.

Many young children with Asperger's Syndrome develop an intense interest in the 'Thomas the Tank Engine' television programmes and merchandise. This is understandable, considering the child's fascination with order, predictability, consistency and symmetry. The carriages must be arranged in a line and a train can only travel along the predetermined track. The parallel railway lines and sleepers are appealing due to their symmetry and regularity. A special feature of the 'Thomas' series is the faces at the front of the engines. If a child has problems deciphering how changes in the position of eyes and mouth convey emotion, then the storyline and movements of the simple faces provide a lesson in emotional expression. The music accompanying the programme is also appealing in terms of its simple repetitive rhythm. Thus, 'Thomas and friends' may become fascinating for many children with Asperger's Syndrome. At this age the child may be starting to learn to read, but not be interested in the conventional books with people as central characters. However, if their first access to reading is via the 'Thomas' series of books and merchandise, then the child's motivation is almost guaranteed. The faces on the engines can also be used in their special programme to learn about emotions.

Should the activity be learning to count and the child has an interest in collecting pictures of flags, then instead of counting blocks, count the number of pictures of flags. If the child has not grasped the basic principles being taught in the lesson, then try and think of examples relevant to the interest. Once the 'magic words' (i.e. reference to the interest) are uttered, the child's attention is captured and maintained. Temple Grandin (Grandin 1988) describes a constructive application of one of her interests:

> Another of my fixations was automatic sliding doors in supermarkets and airports. A teacher might wonder, 'How can I use math, science and English in a door fixation?' At the elementary level, tasks could be simple, such as requesting the door company to send its catalog. Adults might think such a catalog boring, but the autistic child with a door fixation would find it fascinating. Math and geography could be involved by asking the child to find the door company on a map and measure the miles to it from the school.(p.3)

For older children, concentration and effort earn access to the interest. If the child gets all ten sums correct, they have achieved access to the library for ten minutes to read about the interest. If the child has not interrupted the class with questions about their interest for a set period of time, they have earned extra time to access this interest when the lesson is over.

Some interests can eventually become a source of income and employment. A fascination with garden machinery can lead to a job as a contract gardener. An interest in the weather may be the beginning of a career as a meteorologist; an interest in maps could lead to a job as a taxi driver. This practical application of an interest is illustrated by the career of Temple Grandin. She describes (Grandin 1990) how one of her teachers used her special interest:

> Mr Carlock used my fixation on cattle squeeze chutes to motivate me to study science and learn how to use the scientific indexes. He told me that in order to really learn about my interests I had to learn scientific methods and study in school. The psychologists and the counsellors wanted to get rid of my weird interest, but Mr Carlock broadened it away from a narrow fixation into the basis of a lifelong career. Today I travel all over the world designing stockyards and chutes for major meat-packing firms. Recently, I designed a more humane cattle restraint device that

will probably be adopted by most of the major beef-packing plants. Now I am a leader in my field and have written over 100 technical papers on livestock handling. If the psychologists had been successful in taking away my cattle chute fixation, maybe I would be vegetating somewhere watching soap operas. (p.2)

The child may be a talented artist or cartoonist. They could cooperate with a child who is exceptional in writing stories. This child becomes the author and they the illustrator of a book that wins a class or school prize. The child may also benefit from having a personal tutor in their area of interest. This is in order to develop a natural talent that has constructive applications and to increase self-esteem. Teachers and other children will also have greater tolerance of the child's eccentric social behaviour if they recognise an area of accomplishment. Temple Grandin refers to how 'people respect talent even if they think you are weird'(Grandin 1992). Acceleration programmes are now being developed for adolescents with Asperger's Syndrome in areas such as science and foreign languages (Barber 1996). The idea is to be creative – perhaps he could sell his pictures of trains or buildings, become a cricket commentator on television or famous astronomer renowned for his knowledge and enthusiasm.

An interest in computers should be encouraged, not simply as a potential means of employment but to encourage self-confidence and social contact. The child can become a personal tutor to children in their class. In turn, these children may then help the child in other situations in gratitude for their guidance in computers, maths or science. One teenager was an expert on computers but was excluded from the social conversations of the others in his class. As they talked about their parties, vandalism and sexual discovery, he was unable to participate. He looked and felt lonely. However, when the lesson on computers began and several machines 'crashed', his advice and experience were eagerly sought by the others. His posture and facial expression changed. At last he was needed and included. Computer clubs and computer auctions can also be an opportunity to meet like-minded people and for friendship to develop based on a common interest. Thus, the special interest can become the silver lining of the cloud of Asperger's Syndrome.

The interest may also be a source of relaxation and enjoyment, very necessary if one has difficulty coping with the social aspects of daily life. Indulgence in the interest is almost therapeutic. Parents may actually encourage access to the interest when the person is stressed, perhaps at the end of a difficult day at school or work.

The intense interest in a person can be used as an opportunity to learn about feelings, friendships and codes of behaviour. One character quite popular with adults with Asperger's Syndrome is 'Data', who features in the recent *Star Trek* series. He is an android that has remarkable intellectual abilities but longs to be human. He has particular difficulty understanding human courtship, emotions and humour. The difficulties he faces are very similar to those of many adults with Asperger's Syndrome, so no wonder he becomes their hero as they can empathise with his problems. A teacher or parent can use the dilemmas faced by Data to illustrate key aspects of competence in social situations.

Routine

Routine appears to be imposed to make life predictable and to impose order, as novelty, chaos or uncertainty are intolerable. It also acts as a means of reducing anxiety. Donna Williams (1992) describes how:

> I loved to copy, create and order things. I loved our set of encyclopaedias. They had letters and numbers on the side, and I was always checking to make sure they were in order or putting them that way. I was making order out of chaos. Searching for categories did not stop with the encyclopaedias. I would read the telephone directory, counting the number of Browns listed, or counting the number of variations on a particular name, or the rarity of others. I was exploring the concept of consistency. It may have seemed that my world was upside down, but I was looking to get a grip on consistency. The constant change of most things never seemed to give me any chance to prepare myself for them. Because of this I found pleasure and comfort in doing the same things over and over again. (p.38–9)

Thus, the establishment of a routine ensures there is no opportunity for change.

Clinical evidence suggests that the routine becomes more dominant and elaborate when the person has recently experienced changes in the key people in their life, accommodation, daily routine and expectations, or when they display signs of anxiety. The anxiety may also be due to apprehension that they are unsure how to socialise and may make a mistake, and not knowing if there will be a change in routine or expectation. The common reaction to anxiety is to develop a ritual or routine, as in the phrase 'touch wood', or superstitious actions, e.g. not going under a ladder. In psychological jargon, this action operates as a negative reinforcer, i.e. it ends an unpleasant feeling. Thus the establishment of a routine is a secondary consequence of having Asperger's Syndrome and is used as a means of ensuring consistency and reducing anxiety.

But what can you do to prevent the routine becoming excessive? The young child may be determined, even tyrannical, in ensuring the routine is not changed. Parents should insist on compromise and some experience of alternatives. It will help if the young child learns the concept of time using clocks, schedules and a diary. Then they can determine when specific events will occur, and the sequence of activities for the day. Life suddenly becomes predictable. It is important to remember that if a daily schedule is used, it will help to have a separate card for each activity attached to a board using Velcro or Blutak. This is in case there is an unexpected change in the order, and the cards can be rearranged. As the person matures, the insistence on routine tends to diminish, but change is never easily tolerated.

At the end of each school year, there must be a planned transition to the next class and teacher. Several months before the end of the last term, the new teacher can observe the child in the class and the strategies used by their current teacher. When they have the child in their new class, the previous teacher can be consulted for guidance. School administration must also be aware of the problems of rotation of staff, the placement of student teachers and maternity leave disrupting the child's routine.

There will always need to be some reassuring stability maintained in the person's daily life, especially during adolescence, a time of inevitable personal, physical and environmental change. Try and minimise unnecessary disruption during this period and tolerate some routines as the person's means of coping with anxiety. The level of routine imposed by the child or adolescent can be used as a 'barometer' of their level of stress and anxiety. If the routine becomes excessive, then a programme must be devised to restore stability and cope with anxiety. A subsequent chapter of this book will outline a range of strategies that have been used to reduce anxiety for people with Asperger's Syndrome.

Brief Summary of Strategies for Interests and Routines

Special Interests

- facilitate conversation
- indicate intelligence
- provide order and consistency
- become a means of enjoyment and relaxation

Strategies

- controlled access limiting the duration of indulgence
- constructive application to
  - improve motivation
  - become a source of employment or social contact

Routines are imposed to make life predictable.

Strategies

- insist on compromise
- teach the concept of time and schedules to indicate the sequence of activities
- reduce the child's level of anxiety

CHAPTER 5

Motor Clumsiness

One of the first indicators of motor clumsiness is that some children with Asperger's Syndrome learn to walk a few months later than one would expect (Manjiviona and Prior 1995). In early childhood there may be a limited ability with ball games, difficulty in learning to tie shoelaces, and an odd gait when walking or running. When the child attends school, the teacher may be concerned about their poor handwriting and lack of aptitude in school sports. In adolescence a small minority develop facial tics, that is, involuntary spasm of muscles of the face, or rapid blinking and occasional grimaces. All these features indicate clumsiness and specific disturbances of movement.

Clumsiness is not unique to Asperger's Syndrome, and occurs in association with a range of disorders of development. However, research suggests that between 50 per cent and 90 per cent of children and adults with Asperger's Syndrome have problems with motor coordination (Ehlers and Gilberg 1993; Ghaziuddin et al. 1994; Gillberg 1989; Szatmari et al. 1990; Tantam 1991). Thus Corina and Christopher Gillberg have included motor clumsiness as one of their six diagnostic criteria. In contrast, the criteria of Peter Szatmari and colleagues and the American Psychiatric Association make no direct reference to motor coordination. However, the APA has a list of features associated with Asperger's Syndrome that includes the presence of motor clumsiness in the pre-school period and the delay of motor milestones. In addition, the field trials of their criteria have indicated that motor delays and clumsiness are very common in Asperger's Syndrome (Volkmar et al. 1994).

While there continues to be some confusion as to whether motor clumsiness should be a diagnostic criterion, there is no doubt that when it does occur with such children it can have a significant effect on their lives.

What abilities are affected?

There have been several studies that have investigated motor co-ordination in children with Asperger's Syndrome, using a range of standardised tests. These tests include the Griffiths, Bruninks-Oseretsky and the Test of Motor Impairment – Henderson Revision. The results suggest that poor motor coordination affects a wide range of abilities involving gross and fine motor skills. There have also been research studies of more specific motor skills and there is considerable information from clinical observation of movement. The author recommends that children with this syndrome have a comprehensive assessment by a physiotherapist and occupational therapist to determine the nature and degree of any problems with movement. The following are some of the areas where motor clumsiness is apparent, and some strategies to improve particular skills.

Locomotion

When the person walks or runs, the movements appear ungainly or 'puppet' like, and some children walk without the associated arm swing (Gillberg 1989). In technical terms there may be a lack of upper and lower limb coordination (Hallett *et al.* 1993). This feature can be quite conspicuous and other children may tease the child, leading to a reluctance to participate in running sports and physical education at school. A physiotherapist or occupational therapist can devise a remedial program to ensure the movements are coordinated. This may involve the use of a large wall mirror, video recording, modelling and imitating more 'fluid' movements using music and dance. It is interesting that the ability to swim appears least affected, and this activity can be encouraged to enable the child to experience genuine competence and admiration for proficiency with movement.

Ball skills

Catching and throwing accuracy appears to be particularly affected (Tantam 1991). When catching a ball with two hands, the arm movements are often poorly coordinated and affected by problems with timing, that is the hands close in the correct position, but a fraction of a second too late. One study noted the children would often not look in the direction of the target before throwing (Manjiviona and Prior 1995). Clinical observation also suggests the child has poor coordination in their ability to kick a ball. One of the consequences of not being good at ball games is the exclusion of the child from some of the most popular social games in the playground. They may avoid such activities because they know they lack competence, or are deliberately excluded because they are a liability to the team. Thus, they are less able to improve ball skills with practice. From an early age, parents need to provide tuition and practice in ball skills, not to be an exceptional sportsperson, but to ensure the child has basic competence to be included in the games. Some children can be enrolled in a junior soccer or basketball team to improve coordination and to learn how to play specific games. It is also important to have the child's eyesight examined to establish whether wearing glasses improves hand/eye coordination.

Balance

There can be a problem with balance, as tested by examining the ability to stand on one leg with eyes closed (Manjiviona and Prior 1995; Tantam 1991). Temple Grandin (1992) also describes how she is unable to balance when placing one foot in front of the other (tandem walking) i.e. the task of walking a straight line as though it were a tightrope. This may affect the child's ability to use some adventure playground equipment, and activities in the gymnasium. The child may need practice and encouragement with activities that require balancing.

Manual dexterity

This area of movement skills involves the ability to use both hands, for example learning to dress, tie shoelaces or eat with utensils (Gillberg 1989). This may also extend to the coordination of feet and legs as in learning to ride a bicycle. Should the child have problems with manual dexterity, a useful strategy is 'hands on hands' teaching — that is, a parent or teacher physically patterns the child's hands or limbs through the required movements, gradually fading out physical support. This characteristic of movement skills can continue to affect the manual dexterity of adults. Temple Grandin (1984) describes how:

> I can perform one motor activity very well. When I operate hydraulic equipment such as a backhoe I can work one lever at a time perfectly. What I can not do is coordinate the movement of two or more levers at once. I compensate by operating the levers sequentially in rapid succession. (p.165)

Handwriting

The teacher may spend considerable time interpreting and correcting the child's indecipherable scrawl. The child is also aware of the poor quality of their handwriting and may be reluctant to engage in activities that involve extensive writing. Unfortunately, for some children, high school teachers and prospective employers consider the neatness of handwriting a measure of intelligence and personality. The person with Asperger's Syndrome then becomes embarrassed or angry at their inability to write neatly and consistently. The child may well require assessment by an occupational therapist and remedial exercises, but modern technology can help minimise this problem. Children with Asperger's Syndrome are often very skilled at using computers and keyboards and the child could have special dispensation to type rather than write homework and examinations. The presentation of their work is then comparable to the other children. A parent or teacher aide could also act as the child's scribe to ensure the legibility of the child's written answers or homework. In tomorrow's world the ability to write longhand will become much less important, to the great relief of thousands of children with Asperger's Syndrome.

Rapid movements

A recent study noted that while engaged in activities that require motor coordination, such as cutting out shapes with a pair of scissors, a significant proportion of children with Asperger's Syndrome tended to rush through the task (Manjiviona and Prior 1995). They appeared to be impulsive, unable to take a slow and considered approach. With such haste, mistakes occur. This can be infuriating for the child, teacher and parent. The child may need supervision and encouragement to work at an appropriate pace, having time to correct errors. Sometimes the child can be encouraged to slow down by having to count between actions and using a metronome to indicate an appropriate pace.

Lax joints

One of the features examined during a diagnostic assessment is the presence of lax joints (Tantam, Evered and Hersov 1990). We do not know if this is a structural abnormality or due to low muscle tone, but the autobiography of David Miedzianik (1986) describes how:

> At infant school I can seem to remember playing a lot of games and them learning us to write. They used to tell me off a lot for holding my pen wrong at infant and primary school. I still don't hold my pen very good to this day, so my handwriting has never been good. I think a lot of the reason why I hold my pen badly is that the joints of my finger tips are double jointed and I can bend my fingers right back. (p.4)

Should problems occur from lax joints or immature or unusual grasp, then the child may be referred to an occupational therapist or physiotherapist for assessment and remedial activities. This should be a priority with a young child as so much school work requires the use of a pencil or pen.

Rhythm

When Hans Asperger (1991) originally defined the features of the syndrome, he described a child who had significant problems copying various rhythms. This characteristic has been described in one of Temple Grandin's (1988) autobiographical essays:

> Both as a child and as an adult I have difficulty keeping in time with a rhythm. At a concert where people are clapping in time with the music, I have to follow another person sitting beside me. I can keep a rhythm moderately well by myself, but it is

extremely difficult to synchronise my rhythmic motions with
other people or with musical accompaniment. (p.165)

This explains a feature that is quite conspicuous when walking next to a
person with Asperger's Syndrome. As two people walk side by side they
tend to synchronise the movements of their limbs, much as occurs when
soldiers are on parade. Their movements have the same rhythm. The
person with Asperger's Syndrome appears to walk to the beat of a
different drum. This can also affect the person's ability to play an
instrument. They may excel with a solo performance but have
considerable difficulty when playing with other musicians.

Imitation of movements

During conversation there is a natural tendency to imitate the posture,
gestures and mannerisms of the other person. This is more likely to
occur if there is a high degree of rapport or agreement, and occurs
without conscious thought. As previously described, the person with
Asperger's Syndrome may have difficulty in synchronising or mirroring
their movements with those of another person. They may try to
overcome the problem by looking at body movements and immediately
echo them. Clinical experience has identified individuals with
Asperger's Syndrome who will meticulously duplicate the body
postures of the other person to a degree that is conspicuously artificial.
They may be unsure what are the appropriate body postures for the
situation, and imitation is one way of attempting cohesion in
movement. Where this problem occurs it has proved extremely difficult
to identify strategies to learn how to synchronise movements without
them appearing contrived or false.

Recognised Disorders of Movement

Tourette Syndrome

There is increasing evidence that some children and adults with autism
and Asperger's Syndrome develop signs of Tourette Syndrome
(Kerbeshian and Burd 1986, 1996; Marriage and Miles 1993; Sverd
1991; Wing and Attwood 1987). The signs fall into three major
categories: motor, vocal and behavioural. Motor signs are characterised
by repetitive and involuntary movements. Common motor tics include

rapid eye blinking, facial twitches, shoulder shrugging and head, arm or leg jerking. Sometimes complex motor tics develop such as skipping or twitching. All these odd movements can be misinterpreted as 'nervous habits'. Vocal signs include uttering uncontrollable and unpredictable sounds such as repeated throat clearing, grunting, snorting or animal noises such as barking or the shrieking associated with monkeys. Other vocal disturbances included palilalia (repeating one's own words) and echolalia (repeating another's words). All these occur in someone who otherwise has fluent speech. The behavioural signs are obsessive or compulsive behaviours such as continuous making and unmaking of the bed or checking to see if doors are locked. Occasionally the person develops a compulsion to commit a socially obnoxious act, such as touching genitals in public, or outbursts of obscenities that are not relevant to the context or mood. Should any of these characteristics become apparent then it is essential that the person be referred to a psychiatrist or neurologist for diagnosis of this syndrome. Treatment can be quite effective and may involve medication and Cognitive Behaviour Therapy from a clinical psychologist. There are also support groups for families and individuals with Tourette Syndrome.

Catatonia and Parkinsonian features

Signs of catatonia have been identified in association with autism and Asperger's Syndrome (Realmuto and August 1991; Wing and Attwood 1987). With catatonia the person develops odd hand postures and the momentary interruption of ongoing movements. In the middle of a well–practised activity such as eating breakfast cereal or making one's bed, the person becomes motionless and seems to 'freeze' for a few seconds. This is not a petit mal epileptic seizure or daydreaming, but a genuine problem getting limbs and hands moving again.

These movements appear superficially similar to those occurring in Parkinson's disease, a condition that predominantly occurs over the age of 60 (Maurer and Damasio 1982; Szatmari et al. 1990; Vilensky, Damasio and Maurer 1981). The signs are a flat, almost mask-like face, difficulty starting or switching movements, a slow shuffling gait, tremor and muscle rigidity. The author's extensive clinical experience has identified several young adults with Asperger's Syndrome who show a deterioration in movement skills very similar to the pattern in Parkinson's disease. However, it must be stressed that this is extremely rare. Should the person develop signs of catatonia or Parkinsonian features, it is important that they are referred to a neurologist or neuropsychiatrist for a thorough examination of their movement skills. Medication can significantly reduce the expression of these rare movement disorders, and there are simple techniques to help initiate or re-start the movement. For example, another person touching the limb or hand that is required to move can be of considerable help, or working alongside the person with a duplicate set of equipment. Listening to music can maintain movement fluency. It is interesting that certain types of music have proved more beneficial. This is music with a clear and consistent structure and rhythm, as occurs in Baroque and Country and Western music. Physiotherapists have also developed activities for people with Parkinson's disease that could be applied to a younger person.

Cerebellar dysfunction

Recent advances in brain imaging techniques have enabled neuropsychologists and neurologists to examine specific brain structures of people with autism and Asperger's Syndrome. Eric Courschesne originally identified abnormalities of specific areas of a part of the brain called the cerebellum. His pioneering studies have been substantiated by independent research that has included patients who fulfil the criteria for Asperger's Syndrome (Courchesne 1995; El-Badri and Lewis 1993; Hashimoto *et al.* 1995; McKelvey *et al.* 1995). The cerebellum has long been recognised as vitally important in regulating muscle tone, limb movements, timing of movement, speech, posture, balance and sensory modulation. Temple Grandin (1988) has had a Magnetic Resonance Image of her brain which revealed that she too has a cerebellum that is smaller than normal. Thus we now have physiological evidence that confirms the clinical observation of problems with movement. Parents and teachers must be aware that this is a physiological problem, not laziness, and seek remedial activities from experts in the area of movement, particularly physiotherapists and occupational therapists.

Brief Summary of Strategies for Motor Clumsiness

Walking and Running
- improve upper and lower limb coordination

Ball Skills
- improve catching and throwing skills to enable the child to be included in ball games

Balance
- use adventure playground and gymnasium equipment

Manual Dexterity
- try 'hands on hands' teaching

Handwriting
- remedial exercises
- learn to use a keyboard

Rapid Movements
- supervision and encouragement to slow the pace of movements

Lax Joints / Immature Grasp
- remedial programmes from an occupational therapist

Disorders of Movement
- tics, blinking, involuntary movements (examine for Tourette Syndrome)
- odd postures, 'freezing', shuffling gait (examine for catatonia or Parkinsonian features)
- refer the person to the relevant medical specialist

CHAPTER 6

Cognition

Cognition is the process of knowing and includes thinking, learning, memory and imagination. An entire field of cognitive psychology has arisen since the 1950s, and information from this field is now being applied to help our understanding of Asperger's Syndrome. One of the significant advancements has occurred from the research of Uta Frith and colleagues on the hypothesis that children with this syndrome have an impairment in the fundamental ability to 'mind read' (Frith 1989; Happé 1994).

Theory of Mind

From the age of around four years, children understand that other people have thoughts, knowledge, beliefs and desires that will influence their behaviour. People with Asperger's Syndrome appear to have some difficulty conceptualising and appreciating the thoughts and feelings of another person. For example, they may not realise that their comment could cause offence or embarrassment or that an apology would help to repair the person's feelings. The diagnostic assessment used by the author includes asking the child to comment on a series of stories designed to examine whether the child takes account of the thoughts of another person. These stories range from simple examples of figures of speech, such as having a frog in your throat, to a white lie (Happé 1994). The following is an illustration designed to assess the understanding of a white lie:

> Helen waited all year for Christmas because she knew at Christmas she could ask her parents for a rabbit. Helen wanted a

rabbit more than anything in the world. At last, Christmas day arrived, and Helen ran to unwrap the big box her parents had given her. She felt sure it would contain a little rabbit in a cage. But when she opened it, with all the family standing round, she found her present was just a boring old set of encyclopaedias, which Helen did not want at all! Still, when Helen's parents asked her how she liked her present, she said, 'It's lovely, thank you. It's just what I wanted'.

Is it true what Helen said?

Why did she say that to her parents?

Children of primary school age reply to the effect that she did not want to hurt their feelings. Young children with Asperger's Syndrome tend to miss the point and refer to how she could read about rabbits using her new encyclopaedias or are completely puzzled as to why she would lie. Some children with Asperger's Syndrome do provide an appropriate answer, i.e. they give a reply that is based on an understanding of the thoughts or feelings of the characters - but it takes them several seconds to figure out how to answer the question, while other children answer almost instantaneously.

Another story involves double bluff:

> During a war the Red army captures a member of the Blue army. They want him to tell them where his army's tanks are: they know they are either by the sea or in the mountains. They know that the prisoner will not want to tell them, he will want to save his army, and so he will certainly lie to them. The prisoner is very brave and very clever. He will not let them find his tanks. The tanks are really in the mountains. Now when the other side ask him where the tanks are he says, "They are in the mountains".
>
> Is what the prisoner said true?
>
> Where will the other army look for his tanks?
>
> Why did the prisoner say what he said?

A common reply by children with Asperger's Syndrome is that he wanted to tell the truth or was joking, the complex deceit being beyond

comprehension. Clearly a child must have sufficient linguistic and
ıectual capacity to understand the events in these stories, but when
ı abilities are present, one is often astounded that a task so easy for
ır children is so difficult for a child with Asperger's Syndrome.

This characteristic also explains the preference for reading books for
information rather than fictional works, as these portray the characters
and personal experience of people and their interactions. Fiction
emphasises social and emotional experiences, in contrast to nonfiction,
which does not require an understanding of people and their thoughts,
feelings and experiences to the same degree (Garnett and Attwood
1995). This may explain why the child is so bored and disruptive when
the rest of the class is entranced at story time. This characteristic also
occurs with adults. Temple Grandin (1992) has explained that:

> I prefer factual, nonfictional reading materials. I have little
> interest in novels with complicated interpersonal relationships.
> When I do read novels, I prefer straightforward stories that occur
> in interesting places with lots of description. (p.123)

Now that we have recognised this characteristic of 'mind blindness',
what can we do to help the child learn the processes involved? A recent
study used a social skills programme to provide explicit and systematic
instruction in the underlying social-cognitive principles (Ozonoff and
Miller 1995). Scenarios were acted out to help understand the
perspective or thoughts of others, from walking someone who is
blindfolded through a maze (to demonstrate knowledge a person has
that the other does not), to role plays using scenarios similar to the two
previous examples.

There is also research and clinical evidence that the person may have
knowledge about other people's minds, but they are unable to apply
this knowledge effectively (Bowler 1992). They can 'intellectualise'
what a person may be thinking or feeling, but cannot recognise when
such skills are necessary to the situation. This has been called a lack of
central drive for coherence – that is, an inability to see the relevance of
different types of knowledge to a particular problem (Frith and Happé
1994). For example, having taken the favourite toy of another child
without permission and then asked how they think the other child will
feel, the child can give an appropriate answer, yet this thought appeared

not to be in their mind when they took the toy. Thus the knowledge was available, but was not recognised as relevant. Parents and teachers have to teach the child to think of the consequences before they act, a form of 'Stop, Think, Do': Stop and think how the person will feel before you do it. The thoughts and feelings of other people are always relevant.

Profile of Abilities on Intelligence Tests

Elizabeth Wurst was a colleague of Hans Asperger's and was the first to identify a distinct profile of intellectual abilities using standardised tests of intelligence. The person is comparatively good on tests which require a knowledge of the meanings of words, factual information, arithmetic and Block Design. For the Block Design Test the child has to copy an abstract pattern using coloured cubes within a time limit. They are often good at breaking a large geometric pattern into small segments (Frith 1989). For some individuals, the profile can include a significant discrepancy between verbal and performance IQ (Ellis *et al.* 1994; Klin *et al.* 1995), but this can be in either direction.

Unfortunately, there is a tendency for people to judge a person's intellectual ability by their vocabulary and knowledge of facts, and as many children with Asperger's Syndrome are relatively proficient in these areas there can be the assumption the child is remarkably intelligent. However, when the child undertakes a formal intellectual assessment their overall Intelligence Quotient can be disappointingly lower than expected. This is due to their relative weakness on other test items, especially comprehension, picture arrangement and absurdities (Carpentieri and Morgan 1994). On these items the child must have an aptitude with social knowledge. The child can be remarkably competent with recalling information and defining words, but relatively less able at problem solving. As the child ages, tests of intelligence and school work increasingly rely on problem solving abilities.

Intelligence test results can be informative in identifying areas of relative strengths that can be developed for genuine achievement and to increase self-esteem, as well as areas of weakness that may explain why certain activities at school are showing less progress. As the overall profile of abilities on the intelligence test of a child with Asperger's

Syndrome tends to be remarkably uneven, one must exercise extreme caution in using a single IQ figure to express the intellectual abilities of the child. The pattern is more important than the number.

The author recommends that school attainment tests may have to be modified to accommodate the child with Asperger's Syndrome. The important text can be highlighted, seating provided in a position with minimum auditory and visual distraction, and allowance made for problems with handwriting and time taken to write down answers.

Memory

Parents often remark on the child's long-term memory. For example, Albert's parents commented how 'he can remember things when he was so small, like just one incident would happen and nothing would be mentioned about it and a couple of years later he would bring this incident up and remember every detail' (Cesaroni and Garber 1991, p.308). A natural feature of child development is to have difficulty accurately recalling events prior to the development of speech, yet some people with Asperger's Syndrome can vividly recall their infancy. Albert relates:

> I remember when I was one year old I went to Nashville, the air sometimes smelled like firewood. I remember hearing music, it bugged me a lot. I knew I was in a different place, I woke up and smelled the air; it was like a whole bunch of old buildings. (p.307)

Memories can be primarily visual – for example, Candy explained that her 'memories consist of objects rather than people or personal stuff'. The ability for the accurate recall of scenes can extend to remembering whole pages of a book. This eidetic or photographic memory can be extremely helpful in examinations, although the author has known of a university student with Asperger's Syndrome who had been falsely accused of cheating because her examination answers had included perfect and lengthy reproductions of the principal texts for the course. On the positive side, prodigious long-term memory and the accumulation of trivial facts and information on special interests can be an advantage for contestants in television quiz shows such as *Mastermind*. An ability with the game *Trivial Pursuit* led one young man with Asperger's Syndrome to be the prospective champion of the local pub competition. His special interest was old movies. However, he lost by one point in the final when asked when the film *Gone With the Wind* was made. His answer was incorrect, and he calmly accepted his error. His parents could not believe he had made a mistake and conducted some research on the film. Their son had actually given the correct answer, that is, the year the film was *made*, while the answer on the card had been the year it was *released*.

Flexibility in Thinking

The person with Asperger's Syndrome often has difficulty with cognitive flexibility – in other words, they have a one-track mind (Minshow *et al.* 1992). Their thinking tends to be rigid and not to adapt to change or failure. They may have only one approach to a problem and need tuition in thinking of alternatives. With young children it is possible to teach flexibility using games where the child is asked 'What else could it be?' or 'Is there another way you could do that?'. Piles of different shaped plastic blocks could be sorted into different groups according to changing rules (e.g. large versus small, shape, colour or thickness). Ambiguous objects or drawings can become whatever the child can think of. Flexible thinking for older children can be taught using the 'What's Wrong?' cards produced by Learning Development Aids, a manufacturer of educational equipment.[1] Each card depicts a scene that is bizarre or impossible and the child has to identify and describe what is wrong. Another game is 'How many uses can you think of for…?' (e.g. a brick, clothes peg, etc.).

One of the unfortunate characteristics associated with this inflexibility is being less able to learn from mistakes. Parents and teachers may report that the child continues to persevere with the activity, having a 'mental block' and not changing their strategies if they are not working. An often heard phrase is 'he doesn't learn from consequences'. There is now some research evidence to confirm this characteristic (Prior and Hoffmann 1990). One parent said, 'he only seeks help after he has tried his way first'. The child must be encouraged

---

1   Learning Aid Developments, Duke Street, Wisbech, Cambridge, UK.

stop and think of another way or ask for assistance from the teacher
another child. The phrase 'a problem shared is a problem halved' is
...y relevant.

The inflexibility or rigidity in thinking can affect the child's
behaviour in the classroom. A parent commented, 'if he decides
something has to be done, nothing or no one can deter him' and 'you
can't tell him what he doesn't want to hear'. The person seems unable to
cope with being wrong and is infuriatingly rigid when in a discussion
or argument. Once the person's mind is on a particular 'track', they
appear unable to change, even if the track is clearly wrong or going
nowhere. On these occasions it is best to just agree to have a different
opinion.

Once an activity has been learnt, children with Asperger's
Syndrome can fail to transfer or generalise their learning to other
situations. With their 'one-track mind', they may not recognise that
what they have learnt can be used in a wide range of situations. Parents
and teachers may have to teach and remind the child of the different
circumstances relevant to a particular skill. Sometimes teachers and
parents argue that the child's failure in another environment is due to
some inadequacy on the part of other people. It may simply be that the
child has a rigid interpretation of when certain actions are appropriate.

Reading, Spelling and Number Skills

A significant proportion of children with Asperger's Syndrome tend to
be at the extremes of ability in the areas of reading, spelling and
numbers. Some develop hyperlexia, that is, highly developed word
recognition, but very poor comprehension of the words or storyline
(Tirosh and Canby 1993), while others have considerable difficulty
cracking the code of reading. Hans Asperger (1944) referred to how his
original group of children included those with signs of dyslexia and
difficulty learning to spell. In contrast, some were fascinated by
numbers from an early age and were extraordinarily precocious in their
ability to count. For example, he described how a child who had just
started school was asked to work out 5 plus 6. He said:

> 'I don't like little sums, I'd much rather do a thousand times a
> thousand.' After he had produced his 'spontaneous' calculations

for a while, we insisted that he solve the given problem. He then presented the following original, but awkward method: 'Look, that's how I work it out; 6 and 6 equals 12, and 5 and 6 is 1 less, therefore 11'. (p.75)

Another child, Harro, used the following method, which would be more likely to be used by an adult than a child:

Question: 34 minus 12. Answer: '34 plus 2 equals 36, minus 12 equals 24, minus 2 equals 22; this way I worked it out more quickly than any other.'

Question: 47 minus 15. Answer: 'Either add 3 and also add 3 to that which should be taken away, or first take away 7 then 8.' (p.55)

Richard was 17 when he wrote an account of his life and he describes his fascination with numbers from an early age (Bosch 1970):

It all started with an old wall calendar hanging in the baker's shop in the village where we were living. My 'passion' was fired by the large black and red figures, and the three-year-old boy that I was at the time was completely possessed by them. I soon discovered that such 'shapes' were also to be found on doors of houses, on pages in books, and in newspapers. Suddenly my tiny world consisted of nothing but numbers, much to my parents' worry, and they took away my collection of calendar sheets (from the baker) while I was asleep (I used to put them under my pillow). They were not prepared in any way to encourage my thirst for figures, but it happened quite spontaneously that when I was three years old I formed a clear idea of the numbers from 1 to 100, which I can still remember today. I knew clearly what it meant to be three years old: one had been in the world for 1, 2, 3 years. Then I proceeded quite unaided from counting to 'arithmetic'. When I was four, so I am told, I announced triumphantly to my mother, 'Even if you won't tell me, I know how much 4 times 25 is. It's 100, because 2 times 50 is also 100'. I think my mother always used to get quite annoyed when I found out about adult's number secrets. Despite my mother's resistance I pressed on with great tenacity. I can still remember

> that in my second year at school I knew that numbers could go
> up into the billions; this gave me great pleasure. (pp.42–3)

The child's interest in mathematics can lead to an illustrious career as a mathematician. Indeed, the author has met several university professors of mathematics who have Asperger's Syndrome.

An interesting characteristic is that the child with Asperger's Syndrome may not conform to the traditional sequence of stages in acquiring scholastic abilities and may take some time to learn basic skills or acquire precocious or original abilities using an unconventional strategy. The child appears to have a different way of thinking and problem solving. The teacher must be prepared to examine the strategies the child is using and not make a value judgement that they are wrong just because they are dissimilar to other children in the class. They are just different, and for the child, they may be easier than the conventional alternative. Thus it is very important to consider not only what the child can do but how they do it.

Careful observation of such children in the classroom has shown other distinct features. There can be a conspicuous fear of failure, criticism or imperfection. This was explained by Jack, who said (Dewey 1991):

> I am pathologically over sensitive to criticism, I fear that people
> are not going to be pleased with me. I am afraid that if I do the
> wrong thing or say the wrong thing I will undo all the progress I
> have made so far. It could happen as the result of doing
> something by accident. (p.202)

Some children will not try a new activity if they have the slightest suspicion they will fail or there is the merest hint of disappointment. The teacher needs to adopt an encouraging attitude, avoiding any suggestion of criticism. When an error occurs it is also best to avoid the emotion of compassion but quietly and assertively provide guidance, explaining it is not the child's fault, the task really is difficult. Should the child be reluctant to seek help by raising their hand and thereby feeling stupid or possibly being ridiculed by the other children, then a secret code can be arranged between child and teacher. When the child needs help but does not want to draw attention to themselves, they can place an item such as an eraser at a particular position on their desk.

When the teacher sees this secret signal, they can unobt[r]
approach the child and offer assistance. Another feature is to h[
high personal standards that require perfection. These standar[
above the level expected of them by their teacher or other chilure.
There can also be resentment when adults treat them as a child,
especially when being critical or reprimanding. The child often
responds more positively if one adopts the attitude that they are more
mature than their age would suggest.

Children with Asperger's Syndrome are primarily individuals rather
than natural team members. Team situations can be particularly
stressful. For example, one child had to wait his turn to answer a
question in a competition between two classes. He was extremely
anxious that he would provide an incorrect answer and experience
personal and public failure. When his turn came, the teacher asked him
a question that she knew was within his capacity. His extreme anxiety
affected his thinking and speech and he gave an incorrect answer. He
was devastated, despite all the encouragement and consolation from
other members of his team. When people with Asperger's Syndrome
pursue a sport, it is more successfully conducted as a solitary activity
such as golf, fishing, snooker or weight programmes at a gymnasium.

Some children insist on completion and perfection. Candy
described how 'everything has to be exact, nothing can be left
unfinished or incorrect'. Thus the child may remain in the classroom to
finish their work to their standard, long after the other children have
left to go to the playground.

Hans Asperger (1991) referred to how 'we regularly found a
disturbance of active attention' (p.76), and there is clinical evidence to
suggest that Asperger's Syndrome and Attention Deficit Disorder can
both occur with the same child. However, one impression of a lack of
attention is that the child may not be looking at the teacher but is
actively listening. The child is not daydreaming and is very attentive to
what is being said, but not attending to the body language of the
teacher. Another relevant feature is a lack of motivation for activities the
child does not find interesting. If the child has an interest in dinosaurs
and all lessons were about dinosaurs, one has the impression that there
would be no lack of prolonged attention.

A recent study has suggested that such children may have considerable academic achievement in primary school but a deterioration in grades during high school (Goldstein, Minshew and Siegal 1994). Research has shown that this is due to the changing nature of abilities required by the curriculum. In primary school the tasks involve rote mechanical procedures, long-term memory and fairly simple linguistic instructions. At high school, the child is expected to acquire skills in comprehension, conceptualisation, analysis, team work and problem solving. These areas can be relatively less well developed for the teenager with Asperger's Syndrome.

Imagination

With young children one expects a range of imaginative games where the child pretends to be a particular character and dresses accordingly, creates imaginary worlds and uses for their toys and imaginary scenes such as tea parties or cops and robbers are enacted by a group of children. There is something unusual about the imaginative play of children with Asperger's Syndrome. Clinical observations of such children have shown a propensity for imaginative but solitary games and some quite unusual features. For example, a young child with Asperger's Syndrome was playing on his own in a corner of the school playground, pretending to make bread. He had collected grass seeds from the playground, then ground them between stones and was going through the stages from farmer to miller and baker. The other children were fascinated and approached him to join in, but as each child approached they were given a stern instruction to go away. He wanted complete control. Sometimes other children are incorporated into the activity, but the child becomes a dictatorial Hollywood director, insisting on the positions and script of his actors. This solitary imaginative play can appear remarkably creative, but there are occasions when careful observation identifies that the actions and dialogue can be a perfect duplication of the original source. The little figures act the story of Cinderella but the child's tone of voice and script are identical to the teacher's original story to the class. The same routine is carried out day after day. While other children often pretend to be the characters in favourite films and television programmes, the imaginative play of some children with Asperger's Syndrome includes becoming an object rather than a person. One boy spent many minutes rocking from side to side. When asked what he was doing, he replied, 'I'm car wiper blades' – his current special interest. One boy pretended to be a teapot while a girl spent several weeks pretending to be a blocked toilet!

Older children with Asperger's Syndrome create imaginary worlds, especially when they cannot understand or be understood in the real world. This may be one of the reasons for some children's fascination with dinosaurs. Richard describes his dream world (Bosch 1970):

> 'Resteten' was the name I gave to my dream world, a world full of harmony and peace in which nothing evil happened, a world rotating round some distant sun far out in the universe. When I was a small boy, whenever life here on earth seemed difficult and incomprehensible, I liked to retire there to its majestic mountain scenery through which the fast-running Olympia River flowed. This happened very often. For from my earliest childhood on I was different from the others of my age, and for children this is of course sufficient reason to mock, punch, and torture. I was unable to defend myself, because a deep-rooted feeling prevented me from raising my hand to hurt another. As a result mixing with schoolmates, which is for most people an enjoyable part of going to school, was torture for me. Nevertheless, on the very first day I found a friend who was always ready to 'roll his sleeves up' for me. His name, Inno, is more distinctive than he himself ever was; he is a practical, down-to-earth boy who (unfortunately for me) went back recently to live in America where he was born and where he fits in well.

> My present-day love of science was not born simply of a young boy's enthusiasm for figures and arithmetic; it was fed from another source: In my local history and geography lessons I got to know Frankfurt and the Main for the first time. Following the course of the Main on the map, I arrived via the Rhine and its valley at the coast and passed from there over the seas out into the world. I spent more and more time journeying on the map and discovered that there were few, if any, settlements marked in the polar regions. This surprised me, and I now devoted my chief attention to the North and South Poles. From that time on I

followed the explorers into the land of eternal winter. I had always been attracted to places where I thought I would not meet masses of people. Thus at the age of nine I was highly enthusiastic in particular about the bottomless depths of the ocean described in William Beebes' 'Half mile down', the bizarre life forms of bygone eras, which Boelsche describes in his book, 'Leben der Urwelt' (Primeval Life) as well as Picard's adventurous flight into the stratosphere. I then asked myself what lay outside our earth. I found the answer on the star maps and tables of the planets in my father's school atlas as well as in Diesterweg's 'Populare Himmelskunde' (Popular Astronomy). I now became intensely absorbed in this book, while my parents asked themselves whether one should allow a ten-year-old to read such a book. I was particularly interested in the physical structure of the heavenly bodies, less so in the constellations and the times when they could be seen. I got a lot of information from Sir James Jean's book, 'The Mysterious Universe'. A description of a space journey through the sun taught me the structure of atoms, whose electron shells are destroyed up there. The book also led me through the star clusters of the Milky Way to the most distant spiral nebulae. It was only a short step for me from astrophysics to physics. (pp.41–3)

Thus the person can develop a rich, imaginative inner life, a form of escape and enjoyment that can become the first stage of an academic career, or enjoyable pastime. Liam spends hours drawing his own adventure comics about his hero, Supakid, who battles evil and promotes cricket. One woman writes the scripts for an episode of *Star Trek* each day. These are never sent to the producer of the television programme but fulfil her need to slip away from her problems of coping with the real world. Hans Asperger first noted a propensity to develop fantastic stories, and this has been confirmed by later studies (Ghaziuddin, Leininger and Tsai 1995; Tantam 1991). The only negative aspect parents need to be aware of is that some young children with Asperger's Syndrome can have difficulty distinguishing between reality and fiction in books, television programmes and films. They accept the events as reality and can be quite frightened and unable to appreciate that 'it's only a story'. There may also be concern that adolescents spend too much time retreating into their inner fantasy world. If this is the case then parents will need to seek guidance as to how to encourage more social contact and whether this is a sign of a significant illness such as depression.

Visual Thinking

In a recent study, a group of adults with Asperger's Syndrome spent several days wearing a small device that produced a beep at random intervals (Hurlburt, Happ, and Frith 1994). They were asked to 'freeze' the content of their awareness when they heard the beep and record the nature of their thoughts. When this procedure is used with other people, they describe a range of inner thoughts involving speech, feelings, bodily sensations and visual images. However, the adults with Asperger's Syndrome reported their thoughts primarily or solely in the form of images. People with Asperger's Syndrome appear to have a predominantly visual style of thinking. This can have several advantages, as outlined by Temple Grandin (1988):

> My mind is completely visual and spatial work such as drawing is easy. I taught myself drafting in six months. I have designed big steel and concrete cattle facilities, but remembering a phone number or adding up numbers in my head is still difficult. I have to write them down. Every piece of information I have memorized is visual. If I have to remember an abstract concept I 'see' the page of the book or my notes in my mind and 'read' information from it. Melodies are the only things I can memorize without a visual image. I remember very little that I hear unless it is emotionally arousing or I can form a visual image. In class I take careful notes, because I would forget the auditory material. When I think about abstract concepts such as human relationships, I use visual similes. For example, relationships between people are like a glass sliding door. The door must be opened gently, if it is kicked it may shatter. If I had to learn a foreign language, I would have to do it by reading, and make it visual. (p.145)

Temple has recently written a book that explores her visual thinking and how this has affected her life and enabled her to develop quite remarkable skills (Grandin 1995).

The disadvantage of this way of thinking is that so much of school work is presented for a verbal way of thinking. Teachers can help by encouraging visualisation and using diagrams. The child is more able to see solutions to problems than to verbalise solutions. For example, in maths lessons the child can have an abacus on their desk. They can also learn to imagine the principles or events as real scenes. Adults with Asperger's Syndrome have explained how they have learnt history or science by visualising events – for example, running a mental video recording of changing molecular structures. Such children can also have an extraordinary eye for detail which makes their art work quite remarkable.

There are great advantages with this type of thinking. There may be a natural talent for chess and snooker, and the greatest scientist of this century, Albert Einstein, was a visual thinker. He failed his school language tests but relied on visual methods of study. His theory of relativity is based on visual imagery of moving boxcars and riding on light beams. It is interesting that his personality and family history have elements indicative of Asperger's Syndrome (Grandin 1988). There is also evidence that the philosopher Ludwig Wittgenstein and the composer Bela Bartok, both of whom were extremely original in their work, had signs of Asperger's Syndrome (Gillberg 1992; Wolf 1995). Temple Grandin has indicated that, as a child, Vincent Van Gough had traits associated with Asperger's Syndrome (Grandin 1995). When one considers contemporary figures, there has been the suggestion that Bill Gates, the founder of the computer industry leader Microsoft has some characteristics associated with Asperger's Syndrome (Grandin 1995; Ratey and Johnson 1997). The author has met several famous professors and a Nobel Prize winner who have Asperger's Syndrome. Thus the thinking is different, potentially highly original, often misunderstood, but is not defective. Hans Asperger (1979) had a very positive attitude towards those who have the syndrome and wrote:

> It seems that for success in science or art, a dash of autism is essential. For success, the necessary ingredient may be an ability to turn away from the everyday world, from the simply practical,

an ability to re-think a subject with originality so as to create in new untrodden ways, with all abilities canalised into the one speciality. (p.49)

Great advances in science and art have been attributable to people with Asperger's Syndrome.

Brief Summary of Strategies for Cognition

Theory of Mind

- Learn to understand the perspective and thoughts of others using role play and instruction
- Encourage the child to stop and think how the person will feel before they act or speak

Memory

- Apply good recall of factual and trivial information using a quiz and games

Flexibility in Thinking

- Practise thinking of alternative strategies
- Learn to ask for help, sometimes using a secret code

Reading, Spelling, Number

- Examine whether the child is using an unconventional strategy
- If the alternative strategy works, accept and develop it before teaching conventional strategies
- Avoid criticism and compassion

Imagination

- Imaginary worlds can be a form of escape and enjoyment

Visual Thinking

- Encourage visualisation using diagrams and visual analogies

CHAPTER 7

Sensory Sensitivity

For some time we have known that children with autism can be very sensitive to particular sounds and forms of touch yet lack sensitivity to low levels of pain. About 40 per cent of children with autism have some abnormality of sensory sensitivity (Rimland 1990). There is now evidence to suggest that the incidence may be the same for Asperger's Syndrome (Garnett and Attwood 1995; Rimland 1990). One or several sensory systems are affected such that ordinary sensations are perceived as unbearably intense. The mere anticipation of the experience can lead to intense anxiety or panic. Fortunately the hypersensitivity often diminishes during later childhood, but for some individuals it may continue throughout their lives. Parents are often bewildered as to why these sensations are intolerable, while the person with Asperger's Syndrome is equally bewildered as to why other people do not have the same level of sensitivity. The most common sensitivities involve sound and touch, but in some cases the sensitivity relates to taste, light intensity, colours and aromas. In contrast the person may express minimal reaction to levels of pain and temperature that would be unbearable to others.

Sound Sensitivity

Clinical observation and personal accounts of people with autism and Asperger's Syndrome suggest that there are three types of noise that are perceived as extremely intense. The first category is sudden, unexpected noises that one adult with Asperger's Syndrome described as 'sharp', such as a dog barking, a telephone ringing, someone coughing or the clicking of a pen top. The second is high-pitched, continuous noise, particularly the noise from the small electric motors used in kitchen, bathroom and garden equipment. The third category is confusing, complex or multiple sounds such as occur in shopping centres or noisy social gatherings. As a parent or teacher it may be difficult to empathise with the person, as these auditory stimuli are not perceived as unduly unpleasant. However, a suitable analogy for what it may feel like is the natural discomfort many people have to specific sounds such as the noise of fingernails scraping down a school blackboard. The mere thought of this sound can make some people shiver.

The following quotations by people with Asperger's Syndrome or autism illustrate the intensity of the experience. The first is by Temple Grandin (1988):

> Loud, sudden noises still startle me. My reaction to them is more intense than other people's. I still hate balloons, because I never know when one will pop and make me jump. Sustained high-pitched motor noises, such as hair dryers and bathroom vent fans, still bother me, lower frequency motor noises do not.
>
> My mother, my teachers, and the governess did all the right things, except that they were not aware of my sensory problems. If they had known about them, temper tantrums and other bad behaviour would have been reduced even further. When the governess discovered that loud noise bothered me, she punished me when I was bad by popping a paper bag near me. This was torture. Painful or distressing sensory stimulation should never be used as a punishment. I was terrified of anything that might make a sudden unexpected loud noise.
>
> Noise was a major problem for me. When I was confronted with loud or confusing noise I could not modulate it. I either had to shut it all out and withdraw, or let it all in like a freight train. To avoid its onslaught, I would often withdraw and shut the world out. As an adult I still have problems modulating auditory input. When I use telephones at the airport I am unable to screen out the background noise without screening out the voice on the phone. Other people can use telephones in a noisy environment, but I cannot, even though my hearing is normal. When I was a child, noisy birthday parties were unbearable when all the noisemakers were set off. (p.3)

The author endorses Temple's comment that painful sensory stimuli should never be used as a punishment. Darren White (White and White 1987) described how:

> I was also frightened of the vacuum cleaner, the food mixer and the liquidiser because they sounded about five times as loud as they actually were. (p.224)

> The bus engine started with a clap of thunder, the engine sounding almost four times as loud as normal and I had my hands in my ears for most of the journey. (p.225)

The author of the following extract describes auditory sensitivity (Jolliffe *et al.* 1992) in this way:

> The following are just some of the noises that still upset me enough to cover up my ears to avoid them; shouting, noisy crowded places, polystyrene being touched, balloons and aeroplanes, noisy vehicles on building sites, hammering and banging, electric tools being used, the sound of the sea, the sound of felt-tip or marker pens being used to colour in and fireworks. Despite this I can read music and play it and there are certain types of music I love. In fact when I am feeling angry and despairing of everything, music is the only way of making me feel calmer inside. (p.15)

The level of sensitivity can be quite extraordinary. One young child with Asperger's Syndrome was about to leave the clinic when he suddenly and inexplicably became upset, and was unable to explain why. However the author knew of his auditory sensitivity and walked down the corridor in search of the source of the child's distress. In the ladies' toilet someone had switched on the hot air hand dryer, a sound that from the clinic was imperceptible to others, but clearly audible and perceived as too intense to the child.

Albert used his auditory sensitivity to know when a train was due to arrive at the station, several minutes before his parents could hear it. He said, 'I can always hear it, mommy and dad can't, it felt noisy in my ears and body' (Cesaroni and Garber 1991, p306). Another child had a special interest in buses. Before a vehicle was in sight, he could identify the make of the engine. However, he also perceived the unique sounds of the engine of each bus covering that part of the city. Thus, he could identify the number plate of the imminent but invisible bus. He was also reluctant to play in the garden at home. When asked why, he replied that he hated the 'clack-clack' noise of the wings of the butterflies.

One of the features of the acute sound sensitivity is the degree of variation in sensitivity. On some days the sounds are perceived as unbearably intense, while on others they are annoying but tolerable. This variability is described by Darren (White and White 1987):

> Another trick which my ears played was to change the volume of sounds around me. Sometimes when other kids spoke to me I could scarcely hear them and sometimes they sounded like bullets. (p.224)

Perhaps the most common sensitivity is the noise of a barking dog. Shopping trips and family walks become fraught with anxiety as there may be an encounter with a dog; or the person has sleepless nights, aware of a barking dog some distance from the house. Some adults with Asperger's Syndrome have spent their lives avoiding dogs and writing letters of complaint to the local council and noise abatement society.

How does the person with Asperger's Syndrome cope with such auditory sensitivity? Some learn to switch off or tune out certain sounds, as described in a previous quotation from Temple Grandin. Techniques involve doodling, humming or focusing intently on a particular object. Candy described how 'certain noises are difficult to switch out or be around, it has only recently been identified as the culprit to distress'. Thus inattention or odd or distressed behaviour may be a reaction to sounds that the teacher or parent would consider insignificant. Some sounds can be avoided. For example, if the noise of the vacuum cleaner is too intense, it can be used when the child has gone to school. For one child, we observed that she could not tolerate the noise of chairs scraping on the floor of her classroom. This noise was avoided when the legs of each chair had a felt cover. At last she could concentrate on her schoolwork. A barrier to reduce the level of auditory stimulation can be used such as silicone ear plugs, kept in the person's pocket, ready to be inserted when the noise becomes intolerable.

Another strategy is that suggested in the earlier quotation '…when I am feeling angry and despairing of everything, music is the only way of making me feel calmer inside' (Jolliffe *et al.* 1992). We are starting to recognise that listening to music using a headset can camouflage the noise that is perceived as too intense and enable the person to calmly walk round the shopping centre or concentrate on their work in a noisy classroom. Indeed, just having an opportunity to listen to music several times a day can significantly reduce abnormal responses to sound (Bettison 1996). There is also a new technique called auditory training or auditory integration training. This new treatment was originally developed by Guy Berard in France and involves ten hours of listening to specially modulated music (Berard 1993). Preliminary results of independent evaluation are encouraging (Bettison 1996; Rimland and Edelson 1995). However, it is an expensive and as yet unproven treatment, costing more than a thousand dollars for a course of treatment.

It will also help if the cause and duration of the sound that is perceived as unbearable is explained. The Social Stories of Carol Gray are extremely versatile and can be adapted to focus on auditory sensitivity. A social story for a child who was sensitive to the noise of hand dryers in public toilets included a description of the function and contents of the machine, and assurance that it would automatically switch off after a set time.

Clearly it is important that parents and teachers are aware of auditory sensitivity and try to minimise the level of sudden noises, re-duce the background conversation of others and avoid specific sounds known to be perceived as unbearably intense. This will reduce the person's level of anxiety and enable them to concentrate and socialise.

Tactile Sensitivity

There can be an extreme sensitivity to a particular intensity of touch or touching particular parts of the body. Temple Grandin (1984) describes her acute tactile sensitivity when she was a child.

> As a baby I resisted being touched and when I became a little older I can remember stiffening, flinching, and pulling away from relatives when they hugged me. (p.155)

> As a child I did not like the feeling of my legs or arms touching each other, and I wore pyjamas instead of nightgowns. (p.156)

> As a child I wanted to feel the comfort of being held, but then I would shrink away for fear of losing control and being engulfed when people hugged me. (p.151)

For Temple, the forms of touch used in social greetings or gestures of affection were perceived as too intense or overwhelming. Here the avoidance of social contact was due to a physiological reaction to touch, not necessarily an avoidance of being close to or sociable with others.

Particular areas of the body appear to be more sensitive, namely the scalp, upper arms and palms. The child may panic at the hairdresser or when having their hair washed or combed. The child may hate handling certain textures, such as finger paints or playdough. There can also be a reluctance to wear a variety of clothing, as explained by Temple Grandin (1988).

> Some episodes of bad behaviour were directly caused by sensory difficulties. I often misbehaved in church and screamed because my Sunday clothes felt different. During cold weather when I had to walk outside in a skirt my legs hurt. Scratchy petticoats drove me crazy; a feeling that would be insignificant to most people may feel like sandpaper rubbing the skin raw to an autistic child. Certain types of stimulation are greatly over amplified by a damaged nervous system. The problem could have been solved by finding Sunday clothes that felt the same as everyday clothes. As an adult, I am often extremely uncomfortable if I have to wear a new type of underwear. Most people habituate to different types of clothes, but I keep feeling them for hours. Today I buy everyday clothes and good clothes that feel the same. (pp.4–5)

> I cannot tolerate the feeling of skin against skin and prefer to wear long pants to deaden the sensation. (p.13)

The child may insist on having a limited wardrobe to ensure consistency of tactile experience. The problem is having to wash these items, and their durability. Once a particular garment is tolerated, parents may need to buy several of increasing size, to cope with washing and the child's growth.

Fortunately, occupational therapists have devised treatment programmes called Sensory Integration Therapy that may help to reduce tactile sensitivity, or to use the technical term, Tactile Defensiveness. These include massage, gentle rubbing of the area and vibration. Sometimes deep pressure and vestibular stimulation (e.g. spinning and rocking) can help. Temple Grandin (1988) found deep pressure or squeezing was therapeutic.

> I would pull away and stiffen when hugged, but I craved back rubs. Rubbing skin has a calming effect. (p.4)

> I craved deep-pressure stimulation. I used to get under the sofa cushions and have my sister sit on them. Pressure had a very calming and relaxing effect. (p.4)

> As a child, I loved crawling into small, snug spaces. I felt secure, relaxed, and safe. (p.4)

She designed a squeeze machine which enclosed almost her whole body. The machine was lined with foam rubber and provided a firm pressure. She found the firm squeezing created a soothing and relaxing experience that gradually desensitised her.

Sensitivity to the Taste and Texture of Food

Some mothers report that the child was extremely fussy in their choice of food as an infant or during their pre-school years. Sean Barron has explained his perception of taste and texture (Barron and Barron 1992):

> I had a big problem with food. I liked to eat things that were bland and uncomplicated. My favourite foods were cereal – dry, with no milk – bread, pancakes, macaroni and spaghetti, potatoes potatoes and milk. Because these were the foods I ate early in life, I found them comforting and soothing. I didn't want to try anything new.

> I was supersensitive to the texture of food, and I had to touch everything with my fingers to see how it felt before I could put it in my mouth. I really hated it when food had things mixed with it like noodles with vegetables or bread with fillings to make

>sandwiches. I could never, never put any of it into my mouth. I knew if I did I would get violently sick. (p.96)

Fortunately most children with Asperger's Syndrome who have this type of sensitivity eventually grow out of it. It is important to avoid programmes of force feeding or starvation to encourage a more varied diet. The child has an increased sensitivity to certain types of food. It is not a simple behaviour problem where the child is being deliberately defiant. Nevertheless, parents will have to ensure that the child eats an appropriate range of food, and a dietician may provide guidance on what is nutritious but tolerable to the child in terms of texture or taste. Gradually the sensitivity diminishes, but the fear and consequent avoidance may continue. When this occurs, the child can be encouraged to lick and taste rather than chew or swallow new food in order to encourage variety and to test their sensory reaction. They can also be given the opportunity to try new food when relaxed or distracted. However, some adults with Asperger's Syndrome continue to have a very restricted diet consisting of the same essential ingredients, cooked and presented in the same way, throughout their lives.

Visual Sensitivity

A rare characteristic associated with autism and Asperger's Syndrome is a sensitivity to particular levels of illumination, colours, or a distortion of visual perception. Some children and adults report being 'blinded by brightness' and avoid intense levels of illumination. For example, Darren referred to how on 'bright days my sight blurred'. If this occurs, parents and teachers can avoid placing the child in such circumstances, e.g. not sitting at the side of the car that receives the full glare of the sun or at school avoiding a desk illuminated by strong sunlight. Another approach is to use sunglasses, photo chromic lenses and sun visors indoors to avoid intense light or glare. Another option is a work station to screen out excessive visual and auditory stimulation. The author has noted that some adults with Asperger's Syndrome have found Irlen lenses to be beneficial in reducing visual sensitivity.

The intense perception of colours can be recognised in the paintings of some people with Asperger's Syndrome. There are instances where this unique perception has become a source of income as the person becomes an artist renowned for their unusual use of colour.

One unfortunate characteristic is perceptual distortion, as described by Darren White (White and White 1987):

> I used to hate small shops because my eyesight used to make them look as if they were even smaller than they actually were. (p.224)

This can lead to fear or anxiety as a response to certain types of visual experience in the following quotation (Jolliffe *et al.* 1992):

> It may be because things that I see do not always make the right impression that I am frightened of so many things that can be seen; people, particularly their faces, very bright lights, crowds, things moving suddenly, large machines and buildings that are unfamiliar, unfamiliar places, my own shadow, the dark, bridges, rivers, canals, streams and the sea. (p.15)

It is hard to know how to reduce this visual sensitivity. In time we may acquire strategies as effective as those used with auditory sensitivity. At present we can only identify what may be perceived as too intense and try to avoid such experiences.

Sensitivity to Smell

Some people with Asperger's Syndrome report that specific smells can be overpowering (Cesaroni and Garber 1991). Parents will need to be aware that changes in perfume and household cleaning fluids can be perceived as extremely pungent and may have to be avoided.

Sensitivity to Pain and Temperature

The child or adult may appear very stoic, and not flinch or show distress in response to levels of pain that others would consider unbearable. Splinters may be removed without concern, hot drinks consumed without distress. On hot days warm clothing may be worn, or on freezing winter days the person may insist on continuing to wear summer clothes. It is as if the child has a broken internal thermostat.

The lack of reaction to pain can prevent the person learning to avoid certain dangerous actions, causing frequent trips to the local casualty department. Medical staff may be surprised at the audacity of the child or consider the parents negligent. One of the most worrying aspects for parents is how to detect when the child is in chronic pain and needs medical help. Ear infections or appendicitis may progress to a dangerous level before being detected. Dental and menstrual pain and discomfort can occur but not be mentioned. The parents of one child noted he did not seem his usual self for a few days, but was not indicating he was experiencing significant pain. They eventually took him to a doctor who diagnosed a twisted testicle which had to be amputated.

If the child shows minimal response to pain, it is essential that parents are vigilant for any signs of discomfort, check for signs of illness and use the strategies developed for self-disclosure in Chapter 2 to enable the child to tell you of their pain. It is also important to explain to the child why reporting pain is important.

Synaesthesia

This is a rare condition that is not unique to people with Asperger's Syndrome. The person experiences a sensation in one sensory system and as a result experiences a sensation in another modality. The most common expression is seeing colours every time the person hears a particular sound. This is sometimes called coloured hearing. Several people with Asperger's Syndrome have described this unusual phenomenon. For example, Jim (Cesaroni and Garber 1991) described how:

> Sometimes the channels get confused, as when sounds come through as colour. Sometimes I know that something is coming in somewhere, but I can't tell right away what sense it's coming through. (p.305)

He explained that specific sounds are often accompanied by vague sensations of colour, shape, texture, movement, scent or flavour. He also noticed that auditory stimuli interfered with other sensory processes; for example, he had to 'turn off kitchen appliances so that I could taste something'. The experience must be quite bewildering and we have only just begun to conduct research in this area (Harrison and Baron-Cohen 1995).

Brief Summary of Strategies
for Sensory Sensitivity

Auditory Sensitivity

○ avoid some sounds

○ listening to music can camouflage the sound

○ auditory integration training may be helpful

○ minimise the background noise, especially several people talking at the same time

○ consider using ear plugs

Tactile Sensitivity

○ buy several duplicates of tolerated garments

○ Sensory Integration Therapy may be helpful

○ areas can be desensitised using massage and vibration

Sensitivity to Taste and Texture of Food

○ avoid force feeding or starvation programmes

○ only lick and taste new food rather than chew and swallow

○ try new food when distracted or relaxed

Visual Sensitivity

○ avoid intense level of light

○ use a sun visor or sunglasses

Sensitivity to Pain

- ○ look for behavioural indicators of pain
- ○ encourage the child to report pain
- ○ minor discomfort may indicate a significant illness
- ○ explain to the child why reporting pain is important

CHAPTER 8

Frequently Asked Questions

The final chapter attempts to address some of the questions and issues frequently raised by parents such as what causes the syndrome, how to prevent or manage anxiety and depression, what resources are needed and long-term outlook. As we only started to consistently diagnose and investigate this syndrome during the mid-1980s, our knowledge base is limited. However, we do have preliminary information that will end some misconceptions and can offer suggestions for specific problems. Perhaps the first question asked by parents is 'What causes Asperger's Syndrome?'

1. Could it be inherited?

Hans Asperger (1944) originally noticed a ghosting or shadow of similar characteristics in the parents (particularly fathers) of the children he saw, and proposed the condition could be inherited. Subsequent research has confirmed that for some families there are strikingly similar features in first or second degree relatives on either side of the family or the family history includes eccentric individuals who have a mild expression of the syndrome (Le Couteur *et al.* 1996; Bolton *et al.* 1994; Piven *et al.* 1997). There are also some families with a history of children with Asperger's Syndrome and classic autism (Gillberg 1989, 1991; Gillberg, Gillberg and Staffenburg 1992). Thus a brother or sister of the child may be diagnosed as having autism, and further investigation of the family suggests a sibling with Asperger's Syndrome. There are also families with several children or generations with this Syndrome.

Should a parent or relative have had similar characteristics when younger, then they have a unique advantage that is invaluable in helping the child. They know what they are going through. They have empathy, and can offer advice based on their own experiences and strategies they have found to be effective. During those moments when the child feels alone and misunderstood, this family member can explain they have had the same feelings.

Unfortunately, some parents will refuse to acknowledge the syndrome, as to do so means that they must accept they share the same condition. The child is then denied access to understanding and services. It is important that if the features are observed in a parent or near relative, this is recognised as a distinct benefit to the child, and neither relative nor child should be ashamed or embarrassed. Indeed, there are many positive attributes associated with the syndrome.

So far we have not identified the precise means of transmission if the aetiology, or cause, is genetic but we do have some suggestions as to which chromosomes may be involved. Fragile sites have been identified on the X chromosome (Anneren et al. 1995; Gillberg 1989) and chromosome 2 (Saliba and Griffiths 1990) and other chromosomal anomalies such as translocation have been associated with Asperger's Syndrome (Anneren et al. 1995; Gillberg 1989). In particular, children with Fragile X syndrome, a relatively common genetic abnormality, can develop characteristics consistent with Asperger's Syndrome. As our knowledge of genetics improves, we may soon be able to predict the recurrence rate for individual families.

2. Could a difficult pregnancy or birth have been a cause?

In Lorna Wing's (1981) original paper on Asperger's Syndrome, she noted that nearly half of her cases had a history of pre-, peri- and post-natal conditions that might have caused cerebral (i.e. brain) damage. This observation has been substantiated by recent studies. A high incidence of toxaemia in pregnancy was recorded in one study (Gillberg 1989) but, in general, pregnancy may well have been unremarkable (Rickarby, Corrithers and Mitchell 1991). However, the incidence of obstetric abnormalities is high. Although no single factor stands out, a history of obstetric crises, particularly in the later stages of labour, and neonatal problems are recorded with a significant proportion of children with Asperger's Syndrome (Ghaziuddin, Shakal and Tsai 1995; Rickarby *et al.* 1991). There also appears to be a greater incidence of babies who are small for gestational age and mothers in the older age range, that is, over the age of 30 (Ghaziuddin *et al.* 1995; Gillberg 1989). A study of a family who have triplets with Asperger's Syndrome (some parents will have considerable sympathy for this family) suggests that brain damage before, during or after birth may be the primary cause or at least affect the degree of expression (Burgoine and Wing 1983). Thus events that are likely to cause brain damage during pregnancy, birth or early infancy may cause Asperger's Syndrome.

We recognise three potential causes of autism, namely genetic factors, unfavourable obstetric events and infections during pregnancy or early infancy that affect the brain. Another cause of Asperger's syndrome that has yet to be investigated is whether it can be the result of specific viral or bacterial infections before or soon after birth.

3. Is there a specific area of the brain that is dysfunctional?

There is increasing evidence to suggest the frontal and temporal lobes of the brain are dysfunctional. This has been suggested by the results of studies using a range of neuropsychological tests and brain imaging techniques. Studies using the latest technology suggest there may be quite precise areas of the frontal lobes, in particular the medial frontal region or Brodmann's area 8, that, if impaired in early childhood, could produce the pattern of behaviour and abilities of Asperger's Syndrome (McKelvey *et al.* 1995; Fletcher *et al.* 1995; Happé *et al.* 1996; Prior and Hoffman 1990; Rumsey and Hamburger 1988; Volkmar *et al.* 1996). The author has also noted several cases of Asperger's Syndrome where the child had a congenital abnormality of the frontal lobes. There is also some tentative evidence for right hemisphere cortical dysfunction in Asperger's Syndrome that may be similar to a syndrome called Non-verbal Learning Disabilities (NLD) (Ellis *et al.* 1994; McKelvey *et al.* 1995). Thus the scientific evidence suggests specific areas or structures of the brain are dysfunctional.

4. Could we have caused the condition?

A belief that must be discouraged is that Asperger's Syndrome is a consequence of inadequate parenting, abuse or neglect. Unfortunately, parents may initially think the behaviour is somehow caused by some attributes of their parenting or character. Eventually they recognise there is something wrong with the child, not themselves. Nevertheless, relatives, friends and strangers may continue to assume it is due to bad parenting.

Having a child with Asperger's Syndrome can change the parents' social life, conversation and the atmosphere at home. Social contact can be reduced due to repeatedly having to explain and apologise for the child's unusual behaviour. Conversations become pedantic and dominated by the child's interruptions and questions, and the household becomes regimented so as not to distress the child by too much change. The parents may wonder if the Syndrome is infectious as they thought they were perfectly normal before the arrival of the child. One is reminded of the humorous comment: Madness is hereditary – you get it from your children.

The parents' situation becomes more difficult as so few people offer genuine and uncritical support. Some government agencies can also develop the opinion that the child is different due to emotional abuse (Perkins and Wolkind 1991). Parents then avoid contact with service agencies for fear of blame, whereas what they require most are sympathy and support.

Asperger's Syndrome is not caused by emotional trauma, neglect or failing to love your child. The research studies have clearly established that Asperger's Syndrome is a developmental disorder due to a dysfunction of specific structures and systems in the brain. These structures may not have fully developed due to chromosomal abnormalities or have been damaged during pregnancy, birth or the first few months of life.

5. Can Asperger's Syndrome occur with another disorder?

The simple answer to this question is yes. The characteristics of Asperger's Syndrome have been recognised in people with cerebral palsy, neurofibromatosis and tuberous sclerosis (Ehlers and Gillberg 1993; Gillberg 1989; Szatmari et al. 1989), as well as Tourette

Syndrome. In due course we will probably identify other medical conditions that have a risk factor for the pattern of development and abilities of Asperger's Syndrome. Often the other condition is more easily diagnosed and assumed to explain all features. Thus some parents may have to wait some time before both conditions are recognised and treated. Once a single diagnosis of Asperger's Syndrome is confirmed, it may be wise to continue the diagnostic process to examine whether the child has another specific medical condition associated with this syndrome. For example, a recent study identified a child who was diagnosed as having Asperger's Syndrome and subsequently found to have tuberous sclerosis (Rickarby *et al.* 1991).

6. What is the difference between a syndrome and the normal range of abilities and personality?

The normal range of abilities and behaviour in childhood is quite extensive. Many children have a shy personality, are not great conversationalists, have unusual hobbies and are a little clumsy. Indeed, some can become quite abnormally shy (Asendorpf 1993). However, with Asperger's Syndrome the characteristics are qualitatively different. They are beyond the normal range and have a distinct pattern. It is recognised that the condition is on a seamless continuum that dissolves into the extreme end of the normal range. Inevitably, some children will be in a 'grey area' where there is some doubt as to whether their unusual personality and range of abilities have the distinctive quality and degree for a diagnosis using current criteria. These children have a 'ghosting' or 'shadow' of the condition. Nevertheless, the strategies developed for children with Asperger's Syndrome can be modified for such children, who usually benefit from the same programmes. It is noticeable that their rate of progress on such programmes is markedly accelerated.

7. Could the pattern be secondary to a language disorder?

If a young child has difficulty understanding the language of other children and cannot speak as well as their peers, then it would be quite understandable for them to avoid interactions and social play, as speech is an integral part of such activities. Superficially they may have features indicative of Asperger's Syndrome. However, the child with this syndrome has more complex and severe social impairments than secondary shyness or withdrawal and usually has an intense preoccupation with a special interest and greater need for routines. Children with a language disorder also increase their motivation and ability in social play as their language skills and confidence improve.

Asperger's Syndrome is considered as part of the autistic continuum or spectrum and there is one language disorder that borders or overlaps this continuum. Semantic Pragmatic Language Disorder (SPLD) duplicates many of the language features of Asperger's Syndrome and can shade into a milder expression of the syndrome (Bishop 1989; Brook and Bowler 1992; Shields *et al.* 1996). Common features are echolalia, poor conversational turn taking, unusual prosody, difficulty in accommodating the perspective of others, superficially good syntax with odd or inappropriate semantic content. Such children can also have repetitive interests and all have odd social play.

With SPLD the dominant impairment is with language in a social context with relatively minor impairments in social, cognitive, movement and sensory abilities compared to the typical child with Asperger's Syndrome. Such children may initially appear similar to the child with Asperger's Syndrome, but as the child develops, SPLD would be a more accurate diagnosis. Such children need programmes from a speech therapist to improve their language skills and some of the programmes used to help children with Asperger's Syndrome.

8. Can Asperger's Syndrome occur with Attention Deficit Disorder?

Asperger's Syndrome and Attention Deficit Disorder are two distinct conditions, but it is possible for a child to have both. How do you distinguish between them? Perhaps the central feature of Asperger's Syndrome is the unusual profile of social and emotional behaviour. Children with Attention Deficit Hyperactivity Disorder can be notorious for their limited ability to play cooperatively and constructively with other children. However, with ADHD, the children tend to know how to play and want to play, but do so badly. They can be disruptive, destructive and thoughtless, leading to the disintegration of the activity into chaos. Other children may avoid them as they do not want to be associated with bad behaviour. In contrast, the social behaviour of the child with Asperger's Syndrome is qualitatively different and consistent with the distinct profile described in Chapter 2. In addition, children with ADD have a diverse range of linguistic skills and interests, while there is a distinct language and interests profile for those with Asperger's Syndrome. Their interests tend to be idiosyncratic and solitary, in contrast to those children with ADD whose interests are more likely to be conventional for children of that age. Children with both conditions prefer and respond well to routines and predictability, can experience sensory sensitivity and have problems with motor coordination.

As regards attention span, children with ADD demonstrate a consistently limited concentration span. This can vary according to the activity, motivation and circumstances, but almost by definition, there is a deficit in sustained attention. With Asperger's Syndrome there can be a wide range of attention span that is short when involved with social activities but remarkably long when the child is interested in the topic. Here the problem is more one of motivation than a low and fixed upper limit of sustained attention.

Both conditions can be associated with impulsivity but this feature tends to be less of an issue with Asperger's Syndrome. The child with ADD has a propensity to have problems with organisation skills, i.e. has difficulty getting started, switches from one uncompleted activity to another and is forgetful. With Asperger's Syndrome, the profile includes unusual aspects of organisational skills such as unconventional means of solving problems and inflexibility, but in general they are very logical, determined to complete the activity and have good recall of information.

Christopher Gillberg and colleagues in Sweden have studied children with disorders of attention, motor coordination and perception, referred to as DAMP Syndrome, and identified children with Asperger's Syndrome within this population (Gillberg 1983). Recent research suggests that one in six children with Asperger's Syndrome also have clear signs of Attention Deficit Hyperactivity Disorder (Eisenmajer et al. 1996). The two conditions may have specific differences, but there are some similarities and a child can have a dual diagnosis and require treatment for both conditions.

9. Could it be a form of schizophrenia?

Hans Asperger first thought that children with Autistic Psychopathy (his original term for Asperger's Syndrome) had a condition that could develop into schizophrenia. This was more than 50 years ago, and our knowledge of schizophrenia at that stage was extremely limited. Some of the negative signs of schizophrenia such as the poverty of speech and ideas and flattening of affect are very similar (Frith 1991). However, the chances of a person with Asperger's Syndrome developing schizophrenia are marginally greater than for any individual. Indeed, Hans Asperger saw 200 children with the syndrome and only one subsequently developed schizophrenia (Wolff 1995). Recent studies of adults with Asperger's Syndrome suggest that, at most, five per cent develop the signs of schizophrenia (Tantam 1991; Wolff 1995).

The author has seen adult patients referred from psychiatric hospitals with a diagnosis of atypical schizophrenia when on closer examination the person has the developmental history and profile of abilities of an adult with Asperger's Syndrome. Can the signs superficially appear similar to schizophrenia and how do you tell when a real schizophrenic illness occurs?

Some adolescents with Asperger's Syndrome can show a temporary deterioration in abilities, increased social withdrawal, lack of concern for personal hygiene and an intense preoccupation with their interests. This could be interpreted as the period of deterioration that precedes the onset of schizophrenia. Although there are distinct differences between Asperger's Syndrome and schizophrenia, a series of simple errors can lead to a false diagnosis.

The major source of stress in life for the person with Asperger's Syndrome is social contact, and increased stress generally leads to anxiety disorders and depression. The person with schizophrenia has a much broader range of potential stressors and when overly stressed develops clear signs of schizophrenia with hallucinations and delusions.

One of the signs of schizophrenia is the experience of auditory hallucinations. When asked by a psychiatrist – Do you hear voices? – the person with Asperger's Syndrome is likely to reply – yes. This is due to a literal interpretation of the question and not recognising the hidden meaning when this question is asked by a psychiatrist. A subsequent question may be – Do you hear voices of people who aren't there? This can also receive the reply – yes. Further questioning reveals the answer is based on hearing people talking from an adjacent room.

One of the features of Asperger's Syndrome is a difficulty understanding the thoughts of others. A consequence can be to falsely attribute malicious intent. The incident may have been an accident but interpreted as personal and intentional. The person may actually overhear derogatory comments about their personality or social abilities. This can lead to being highly suspicious of others to a level that can resemble paranoia. However, this is due to problems with acquiring a 'Theory of Mind' and an accurate perception of intention rather than a distortion of reality.

People with Asperger's Syndrome may have unusual qualities to their language skills that superficially resemble the speech and thought disorder associated with schizophrenia. Such people often vocalise their thoughts in social settings or in private, for example while on the toilet or in the bathroom. They may be replaying the conversation they have been involved with during the day. There can also be a tendency to talk in the third person, i.e. not using 'I' as the appropriate personal pronoun, but referring to themselves as he (or she). This makes the monologue distinctly odd, especially when the replayed 'conversation' involves intense emotions. Another feature of Asperger's Syndrome is delayed emotional maturity. Thus older teenagers and young adults can maintain a belief in the supernatural that seems immature and childlike. Their explanations for events may include magic and fantasy, and they have difficulty distinguishing fact from fiction. This unusual or immature view of reality can be confusing to the clinician who is not aware of this aspect of Asperger's Syndrome, and may view it as evidence of delusions.

It is easy to see how a false diagnostic trail is created. Unfortunately, there is likely to be a significant proportion of people diagnosed as having treatment-resistant or atypical chronic mental illness, especially schizophrenia, who will eventually be recognised as having Asperger's Syndrome (Ryan 1992). The original diagnosis of schizophrenia may have been questionable, but at the time the person or family needed professional help and psychiatric services were the only agencies available. Treatment was likely to have been sedation and institutional care rather than improving social behaviour and understanding.

Finally, clinical experience suggests that a small minority of young adults with Asperger's Syndrome can develop the genuine signs of schizophrenia. However, such episodes tend to be brief and often linked to a particular stressful event such as an examination. Should parents recognise genuine signs of delusions, or hallucinations, then it is essential that the person is referred to a psychiatrist who is knowledgeable in Asperger's Syndrome.

10. What is the difference between High Functioning Autism and Asperger's Syndrome?

We recognise that there are clear differences between children with Asperger's Syndrome and autism, as originally defined by Leo Kanner, on measures of social interaction, language and long-term development (Szatmari *et al.* 1995), but is Asperger's Syndrome different from High Functioning Autism?

We have known for many years that some children have the classic features of autism in early childhood, but later develop the ability to talk using complex sentences, develop basic social skills and an intellectual capacity within the normal range. This group was first described as having High Functioning Autism, a term that remains most popular in the United States. The author has noted that this term is most likely to be used for individuals who had a diagnosis of autism in their early childhood. It is less likely to be used for children whose early development was not consistent with classic autism.

What is the difference between these two terms and do they describe different attributes? There have been numerous studies that have tried to determine if a distinction can be drawn between the two (Eisenmajer *et al.* 1996; Kerbeshian, Burd and Fisher 1990; Manjiviona and Prior 1995; Ozonoff, Rogers and Pennington 1991; Szatmari, Burtolucci and Bremner 1989). At present, the results suggest there seems to be no meaningful differences between them. They are more the same than they are different.

The term High Functioning Autism (HFA) has been used for some time in English speaking countries and continues to be used by some clinicians as their preferred diagnostic label. This is due to a number of factors, particularly the policies of government organisations that provide services, and the lack of knowledge and training in the diagnosis of Asperger's Syndrome. Some agencies readily provide funds for a child diagnosed as having autism, but the term Asperger's Syndrome has yet to be included as an approved condition with associated entitlements. Clinicians may then be reluctant to use the term as this can delay or inhibit access to services. Another factor is the availability of literature and training for clinicians on how to diagnose the syndrome, and the conservatism of certain individuals. Thus the same child may be diagnosed as having HFA in one locality but having Asperger's Syndrome in another.

Both autism and Asperger's Syndrome are on the same seamless continuum and there will be those children who are in a diagnostic 'grey area' where one is unsure which term to use. In due course we will be able to identify the boundaries between autism and Asperger's Syndrome. At present one may use a practical approach: use the diagnosis that provides the services.

11. Do girls have a different expression of the syndrome?

The boy to girl ratio for referrals for a diagnostic assessment is about ten boys to each girl (Gillberg 1989). However, the epidemiological evidence indicates the ratio is 4:1 (Ehlers and Gillberg 1993). This is the same ratio as occurs with autism. Why are so few girls referred for a diagnosis?

So far there have not been any studies that specifically investigate any variation in expression of features between boys and girls with Asperger's Syndrome, but the author has noticed that in general boys tend to have a greater expression of social deficits with a very uneven profile of social skills and a propensity for disruptive or aggressive behaviour, especially when frustrated or stressed. These characteristics are more likely to be noticed by parents and teachers who then seek advice as to why the child is unusual. In contrast, girls tend to be relatively more able in social play and have a more even profile of social skills. The author has noticed how girls with Asperger's Syndrome seem more able to follow social actions by delayed imitation. They observe the other children and copy them, but their actions are not as well timed and spontaneous. There is some preliminary evidence to substantiate this distinction from a study of sex differences in autism (McLennan, Lord and Schopler 1993).

Girls with this syndrome are more likely to be considered immature rather than odd. Their special interests may not be as conspicuous and intense as occurs with boys. Thus, they can be described as the 'invisible' child – socially isolated, preoccupied by their imaginary world but not a disruptive influence in the classroom. Although girls are less likely to be diagnosed, they are more likely to suffer in silence.

An important issue for girls is that during adolescence the usual basis for friendship changes. Instead of joint play with toys and games using imagination, adolescent friendship is based on conversation that is predominantly about experiences, relationships and feelings. The young teenage girl with Asperger's Syndrome may want to continue the playground games of the primary school and starts to reduce her contact with previous friends. They no longer share the same interests. There is also the new problem of coping with the amorous advances of teenage boys. Here conversation is acceptable but concepts of romance and love as well as physical intimacy are confusing or abhorrent.

In an attempt to be included in social activities, some teenage girls have described how they have deliberately adopted a 'mask' like quality to their face. To others at school they seem to continuously express a smile, but behind the mask the person is experiencing anxiety, fear and self doubt. They are desperate to be included and to please and appease others but cannot express their inner feelings in public.

The author has observed girls with the classic signs of Asperger's Syndrome in their primary school years progress along the autism/Asperger's Syndrome continuum to a point where the current diagnostic criteria are no longer sensitive to the more subtle problems they face. The author's clinical experience would suggest that girls have a better long-term prognosis than boys. They appear to be more able to learn how to socialise and to camouflage their difficulties at an early age. This is illustrated by Vanessa's poem.

Ironing Out the Wrinkles

Life was once a tangled mess.
Like missing pieces, in a game of chess.
Like only half a pattern for a dress.
Like saying no, but meaning yes.
Like wanting more, and getting less.
But I'm slowly straightening it out.

Life was once a tangled line.
Like saying yours, and meaning mine.
Like feeling sick, but saying fine.
Like ordering milk, and getting wine.
Like seeing a tree, and saying vine.
But I'm slowly straightening it out.

Life is now a lot more clear.
The tangles are unravelling,
And hope is near.
Sure there are bumps ahead.
But no more do I look on with dread.
After fourteen years the tangles have straightened.

(Vanessa Regal)

The residual problems are described by individuals as 'feeling different to others'. Although their social interactions with others superficially appear natural, they consider they are mechanical and not intuitive. They remain confused as to how others share intimacy and maintain friendships with so little thought.

12. How can you reduce the person's level of anxiety?

Previous sections of this book have explained why the person with Asperger's Syndrome is susceptible to anxiety. Any social contact can generate anxiety as to how to start, maintain and end the activity and conversation. School becomes a social minefield; at any moment you can put a foot wrong. The natural changes in daily routines and expectation cause intense distress while certain sensory experiences can be unbearable. All these factors combine to make the person anxious.

For some, the level of anxiety fluctuates and arrives in 'waves' with periods of intense panic, followed by a period of relative calm. Reassurance over a particular issue may help but one has the impression that the person has inherent feelings of anxiety looking for a cause. Once this has been rationalised, the anxiety 'floats' to another rationalisation or justification. The person may cope with their anxiety by retreating into their special interest and the level of preoccupation can be used as a measure of the person's degree of anxiety. The more anxious the person, the more intense the interest. When anxious the person is also more rigid in their thought processes, and more insistent on routines. Thus, when anxious the person increases their expression of Asperger's Syndrome, yet when happy and relaxed one may have to be very skilled to recognise the signs.

For minor levels of anxiety a simple stress management programme can be effective. Parents and teachers commence the programme by noting the signs of the child's increasing level of anxiety. They may start by rocking gently, then become tense or very rigid in their thinking. These are observable signs based on the behaviour and actions of the individual but certain events may be known to trigger anxiety, for example uncertainty as to whether an eagerly anticipated event will occur, a birthday party or an examination at school. When internal or external signs indicate imminent or increasing anxiety, there are several options – activities that encourage relaxation, achievement or distraction, or activities that require physical energy to 'burn up' their tension and anxiety.

With low levels of anxiety, relaxation, achievement and distraction are the preferred options. Relaxation can be encouraged by listening to appropriate music (i.e. not heavy rock music), providing a sanctuary without social or conversational interruption, and using a relaxation programme that uses massage, deep breathing and thinking positive thoughts. Indulgence in a favourite interest can also help to distract and relax the person. Another option is to encourage achievement by using the computer, going through school material that the person finds interesting and easy, and distracting the person by activities such as tidying up to restore order and symmetry.

When the person is becoming increasingly anxious or agitated, the alternative option may be to start an activity that requires physical exertion. For young children, this could be to use the swing or trampoline, ride their bicycle, or go for a long walk. The dog may welcome the exercise. Teenagers could be given specific physical chores in the house or garden. Jumping on a trampoline can be an appropriate activity for all ages. A woman with Asperger's Syndrome had chronic anxiety and described how she felt 'wound up' after her day at work. When we discussed the physical activities she could do, she said she longed to be able to jump on a trampoline but couldn't because she felt she would be viewed as mad or eccentric by her neighbours. She was determined to be seen as conventional. However, we suggested she explained to others that this was part of her keep fit and dieting programme prescribed by her doctor. With this 'prescription', she could indulge in an activity she found enthralling and therapeutic.

These strategies are simple procedures for managing anxiety and stress, but with Asperger's Syndrome the most stressful activity is having to socialise. If social play is a major stressor that affects the child's mood, then they may require an alteration to the schedule of activities in the school day or the amount of time they spend in the classroom. Other children enjoy the social and unstructured aspects of break time, but such circumstances are extremely stressful for the child with Asperger's Syndrome. On the one hand it is important that they learn to play with others; on the other hand, the stress can affect the child's level of anxiety, competence and tolerance during subsequent lessons. A suggestion that has proved valuable with some children is to have the first half of the break period in free play with the other children, but for the second half the child is able to engage in solitary and constructive activities such as going to the library to read about their special interest or using the computer in the classroom. After such solitary but relaxing pursuits the child is better able to cope with the social aspects of the classroom.

For young children, and even some teenagers and adults, it is necessary to have islands of solitude throughout the day. Candy explained how at work she was anxious about socialising at break times, but said 'Crosswords are a blessing – for to become absorbed in one during breaks keeps people at the required distance.' The teacher may identify specific responsibilities that enable solitude, for example going to the school office with a message. The envelope may only contain the instruction to the secretary to thank the child for delivering the message, and ask them to return to the class.

Some children are anxious about not appearing stupid or being the centre of attention and may be reluctant to publicly ask the teacher for assistance. If the child is anxious about asking for assistance then a secret code can be established between child and teacher, such as placing a particular item (e.g. a pencil sharpener) on a particular position on their desk, indicating that they require help. The teacher can then provide guidance without the child feeling conspicuous.

There has been some success in reducing anxiety and increasing scholastic attainment by scheduled breaks during the term, part-time enrolment or home tuition. Parents and teachers may be aware that the term has been too long for the child and they are showing signs of chronic anxiety. As much as a child who is physically ill may have a few days off school, the child with Asperger's Syndrome may need a few days off to relax, enabling them to cope till the end of term. Some children are enrolled only for morning classes and return home in the afternoon. School work is undertaken during the afternoon, but alone and supervised by a parent. When anxiety is extreme, full-time home tuition has proved successful, especially with teenagers. The circumstances for each application for home tuition must be examined carefully, ensuring adequate access to trained teachers and preventing complete isolation from other children. However, this approach can be a constructive alternative to strong medication and possible admission to a psychiatric unit. This option of home tuition has proved particularly beneficial for some teenagers with a secondary diagnosis such as depression or Obsessive Compulsive Disorder.

Prolonged periods of severe anxiety can lead to a secondary psychiatric condition such as Obsessive Compulsive Disorder. For example, the person may develop a compulsion to wash their hands due to a fear of contamination. These actions operate as a means of reducing their anxiety. Should the level of anxiety be extreme then professional help is required from a psychiatrist and clinical psychologist. There is a range of medication for anxiety disorders that has been used for people with autism and Asperger's Syndrome (Gordon *et al.* 1993; McDougle, Price and Goodman 1990; McDougle *et al.* 1992; Szabo and Bracken 1994). Temple Grandin (1990) describes how:

Shortly after my first menstrual period, the anxiety attacks started. They were like a constant feeling of stage fright. I often tell people, just imagine how you felt when you did something really anxiety provoking, such as your teacher's certification exam. Now just imagine if you felt that way most of the time for no reason. I had a pounding heart, sweaty palms and restless movements.

...The nerves followed a daily cycle and were worse in the late afternoon and early evening; they subsided late at night and early in the morning. They also had a tendency to be worse in the spring and fall.

...I read in the medical library that antidepressant drugs were effective for treating patients with endogenous anxiety and panic. . . . These pills have changed my life. (pp.9–11)

Severe anxiety with associated depression and ritualistic behaviour can be significantly reduced by a new range of medication – the Selective Serotonin Reuptake Inhibitors.

Cognitive Behaviour Therapy can also be used by a clinical psychologist to treat severe anxiety and panic attacks, as well as fear and anxiety associated with a specific situation such as exams or panic associated with seeing a particular object or animal. The therapy involves changing the way the person thinks about and reacts to anxiety. The approach is to treat the fear much as one would treat the fear of anyone who has a phobia. The fear of certain animals is quite common; many people fear snakes, spiders, rats, etc. Children with Asperger's Syndrome can fear dogs, not because of a fear of being attacked, but the noise of the barking is perceived as too intense and unbearable. Some children with the syndrome can develop anxiety in association with inanimate objects such as mannequins in a shop window or house plants. The child has an intense panic reaction to these objects but cannot explain why they are so distressing.

If a person was receiving treatment for a fear of spiders, they would be encouraged to relax (the opposite of anxiety or fear) and think of a dead spider some distance away, maintaining the relaxation through the encouragement of the clinical psychologist. Gradually the person would become accustomed to thinking of and eventually being close to larger spiders, until the anxiety reached a natural level. This approach is called desensitisation, and has been used with children with Asperger's Syndrome. For the child with the fear of house plants, we chose a time when he was relaxed, namely at the end of the day and after his bath, and gradually encouraged him to accept a very small house plant, initially at the other end of the room, then on a table beside him. This simple procedure reduced his anxiety, but we encountered a problem common to children with Asperger's Syndrome, namely a difficulty in generalising learning from one situation to another. His mother explained this quite succinctly by saying, 'He gets used to the one you train him on, but any new plant makes him go berserk!' Nevertheless, there has been some success using something enjoyable to eat, such as chocolate or ice cream, or thinking positive thoughts in association with the feared object or situation.

Another approach which relies more on thinking or cognitive skills is to explain and demonstrate to the child that they can control their anxiety. This treatment requires the expertise of a clinical psychologist trained in Cognitive Behaviour Therapy and a modification of this therapy to include a greater emphasis on using imagery and visual rather than verbal reasoning. For example, a child can use a pencil to draw a simple picture of themselves with a thought bubble that represents their anxiety. They can then use an eraser to remove the content of the bubble and replace it with an alternative, more pleasant thought. They are then more able to conceptualise changing their thoughts. While the more simple approach of desensitisation can be undertaken by parents or teachers, both these treatment programmes are time consuming but are preferable to solely relying on medication to reduce anxiety.

13. Is the person likely to become depressed?

In Lorna Wing's original paper (1981), she remarked on the high incidence of depression or affective disorder in adults with Asperger's Syndrome. Clinical experience has also confirmed there is a greater risk for depression, with up to 15 per cent of adults having had a period of depression (Tantam 1991) and the genuine risk of suicide (Wolff 1995). During early childhood the person may be less concerned about their differences to other children. Their life revolves around their family and the teacher, with social contact with others having limited value or interest. During adolescence they start to become more interested in socialising with others and become acutely aware of their difficulties. The least intellectually able child in the class can be socially skilled, a leader and a comedian; yet despite their intellectual ability, when the person with Asperger's Syndrome tries to have friends, be the centre of attention or tell jokes, they are excluded, teased or ridiculed. This is the most common cause of depression – wanting to be like others and to have friends, but not knowing how to succeed.

Thus the cause of the depression may be an understandable reaction to having Asperger's Syndrome, but in some cases there may be a biological predisposition. Research studies have suggested that there is a marginally greater incidence of depression or manic depression (bi-polar affective disorder) in families that have a child with autism or Asperger's Syndrome (DeLong and Dwyer 1988). One may argue that having such a child might make you feel depressed, but the studies have controlled for this factor.

In most cases there are classic signs of depression with clear changes in mood, appetite, sleep, and suicidal thoughts and actions. However, the diagnosis of depression may not be straightforward, as the person may have a limited range of emotional expression and a history of flat affect. The depression may also be expressed as aggression or alcoholism. The person can become very introspective and critical of themselves in relation to the day's events, and seek relaxation and emotional blunting by using alcohol as a form of self-medication. Should one suspect the person is depressed, then it is essential that they obtain a referral to a psychiatrist knowledgeable in Asperger's Syndrome, and obtain treatment. The author has known several individuals who have committed suicide.

One of the features of Asperger's Syndrome described in Chapter 2 is a tendency to laugh or giggle in circumstances when one would anticipate an expression of embarrassment, discomfort, pain or sadness. There have been instances of grief over the death of a member of the family being expressed by laughter or mania (Berthier 1995) or even indifference. This is due to the inability to express appropriate and subtle emotions. This unusual reaction is not evidence of callousness or mental illness. The person needs understanding and tolerance of their idiosyncratic way of expressing their grief.

The treatment for depression involves conventional medication, but should also include programmes to deal with the origin of the depression, usually poor social skills, lack of friends and limited success at school or work. The high incidence of depression in adults may be a reflection of the lack of understanding and remedial tuition that this generation experienced during childhood. It is anticipated that the current generation of children who have had early and accurate diagnosis as well as effective programmes in social skills will be less vulnerable to depression as teenagers or adults. Such programmes may be an 'inoculation' against depression. Certainly the person who is depressed due to a lack of friendships and employment needs guidance in learning social skills, job interview techniques and access to meeting people with similar interests and values. These strategies may take time but are likely to prevent the recurrence of depression.

14. How do you control the person's temper and anger?

This book has outlined the many sources of stress for the person with Asperger's Syndrome. Some will react to this by becoming anxious, some by feeling depressed, while others become angry and rage against the frustrating incidents in their day. Some individuals externalise their feelings and tend to blame others when things go wrong. Those who externalise their feelings describe having great difficulty in controlling their temper, as illustrated in Daniel's poem:

> **My Greatest Fear is Myself**
> My greatest fear is myself.
> Control is not absolute: a constant struggle to maintain
> it drains my strength.
> I am always tired: I never get enough sleep.
> Events beyond my control happen around me: I do
> things that scare me. If I'm confused or angry or tired,
> I slip up and my body takes over.
> Watching your life like a void is scary. It takes an
> effort of will to take control again and not just let it
> happen.
> I'm afraid of what I feel. Emotion weakens my control,
> making its grip easier to break.

When I think, I sometimes think of letting go, just
letting it all slip away. It hurts fighting all the time.
I just want peace and rest.

(Daniel Woodhouse)

There may be no particular rationalisation or focus – just an aggressive mood or an excessive reaction to frustration or provocation. The provocation can be deliberate teasing by other children, or being 'set up' as a form of live theatre enjoyed by the children who do not get into trouble. The author has found that children with Asperger's Syndrome seem to evoke the maternal or predatory instinct in others. Children with this syndrome often lack subtlety in retaliating. Other children would wait for an appropriate moment to respond without being caught. The child with Asperger's Syndrome can also lack sufficient empathy and self-control to moderate the degree of injury. They are in a blind fury that gets them into trouble. The teacher sees the child being aggressive and may not be aware of the taunts that precipitated the anger.

Chapter 2 included a section on strategies to help the child understand the nature and expression of specific feelings, particularly anger. These strategies can be used with the young child whose anger causes concern for parents and teachers. Another activity is to encourage self- control and to consider alternative options. Self-control can be strengthened by the traditional approaches of stopping and counting to ten, taking a deep breath and reminding oneself to keep calm. Specific relaxation techniques can be practised and the child taught the cues when they must calm down and relax. It is also important to explain the alternative option to hitting the other person. The child can use words, not actions, to express their anger, or walk away, ask the other person to leave them alone, or seek an adult for help or to be a referee.

The child's level of stress may have been increasing for some time, and one incident becomes the trigger that releases feelings that have long been suppressed. The destruction or assault can leave the person relieved at having discharged their stress in one brief episode of anger. Thus, the behaviour becomes negatively reinforced. It helps end an unpleasant feeling. Unfortunately, some males with Asperger's Syndrome have an authoritarian outlook on life with a rigid hierarchy where males are dominant over females. Thus, girls or mothers may be targeted when the person feels angry, as a means of releasing tension and agitation. They are also less likely to retaliate. When the incident is over, the person with Asperger's Syndrome can be visibly relaxed, but confused as to why everyone else continues to be so distressed.

If the person's temper or anger is of concern, there are several strategies to consider. The first is to construct a list of the signs that indicate the person is becoming increasingly stressed. This can include an increase in swearing, bombastic gestures, rigid thinking and desire for immediate gratification. Parents and teachers can compare notes relevant to different situations. Once these signs are recognised, the person's attention must be drawn to their actions and behaviour. They are often the last to recognise how their mood and tolerance are deteriorating. Then construct a list or 'menu' of activities to reduce low levels of stress. Listening to music can be extremely successful, as in the term, 'Music soothes the savage breast'. Parents can encourage the person to relax and close their eyes while they describe and the person visualises a relaxing scene. Other options include massage, or a soothing bath and plenty of reassurance and compliments. These procedures are designed to take the person's mind away from angry thoughts. Sometimes having a sanctuary and a period of solitude will help. One must be careful with the question, 'What's the matter?', as the person may have difficulty explaining the causes of their increasing anger. When the person can maintain self control, they may be able to explain the reasons for their mood, but sometimes focusing on the cause can precipitate more anger. Parents and teachers will learn when it is tactful not to ask.

Should the level of agitation become greater, then another strategy is to 'burn up' the tension and anguish with an activity that requires vigorous physical involvement. Activities such as going for a run, or cycling, can leave the person invigorated and in a more optimistic mood. The author has found that activities that involve creative destruction are particularly effective. If the person feels better after they have damaged or destroyed something, then ensure this becomes a productive activity. Crushing empty cans and cardboard boxes for recycling or tearing old clothing to make rags can be undertaken by younger children while adults can try activities such as chopping wood.

The above are general strategies to reduce and channel aggression into constructive activities. What can you do in response to a specific incident? The first point is that by becoming equally angry you will inflame the situation. One mother described how 'if I get angry with him it's like throwing petrol on a BBQ'. Try to remain calm and rational – a model of what the child should be doing. If the person will tolerate discussion of why they are so angry, try to discover the cause. For example, if it is in response to teasing, then both parties should be part of the discussion. An apology (sometimes from both parties) will help, but for younger children it is important they learn to be sincere and genuine in considering the person's feelings. One strategy the author has used is ensuring the child donates or does something as compensation to the child they hurt. It is important to learn to express remorse by deeds as well as with words. Perhaps they should now share the chocolate biscuits they were going to have at lunchtime. It is also important to explain to the child what they can do should the situation happen again with comments such as, 'Next time he pokes his pencil in your back, tell me and I will help you deal with it'. Such children are not skilled in the gentle art of persuasion and can only manipulate others by relying on intimidation and physical force. It is essential that the child learns alternative preferably verbal and subtle ways of achieving their goal.

For older children, the Comic Strip Conversations by Carol Gray can be an excellent means of debriefing the person, and using the incident as an opportunity to learn the perspective of others and to consider alternative solutions. A story board approach is used with a frame for each stage in the sequence of events. The colour chart for emotions developed by Carol can help explain feelings, and the 'barometer', described in Chapter 2, can be used to explain how the expression was too severe and what would be more appropriate and subtle words and actions. The cartoons are drawn in an atmosphere of trying to find out what happened and to understand the thoughts and feelings of each participant without fear of recrimination, which could affect the person's attitude and receptivity. Consequences will become an issue, and having Asperger's Syndrome is not a licence to behave irresponsibly, but it is important for all information and perspectives to be available before appropriate consequences are considered.

Medication can be used as an option to treat anger. The availability of a quick acting sedative can be appealing. As a matter of expediency for a particularly stressful period, medication can be appropriate. However, it is only a temporary measure and children and adults with autism and Asperger's Syndrome are particularly vulnerable to the long- term side effects of medication prescribed as a sedative, especially the antipsychotics. Medication can be valuable but must be prescribed to treat specific signs, be reviewed regularly and be of short duration.

There are rare cases where the aggression occurs out of the blue, is brief and intense, and for no apparent cause (Baron-Cohen 1988). These spontaneous and unpredictable episodes are of great concern for parents, and may be related to neurological factors, especially complex partial seizures. Should these occur, then the person should be referred to a neurologist specialising in developmental disorders for further investigation and treatment.

Finally, when considering anger it is important to recognise that such behaviour is not a universal feature of Asperger's Syndrome. Indeed there are many children with this syndrome who seem almost devoid of anger, even under intense provocation. Such children can be extremely vulnerable to physical abuse and exploitation from 'friends'. They need to learn to be assertive and to cope with the playground 'jungle'.

15. What are the changes we can expect during adolescence?

The physical changes of adolescence are likely to occur at the same age as for their peers, but young people with Asperger's Syndrome may be confused by such changes. One teenage boy continued to maintain a high-pitched or falsetto tone to his voice long after it had 'broken' (a term likely to add to the confusion of the person with Asperger's Syndrome). When asked why he talked in such an unusual tone of voice he replied, 'I don't like the sound of my voice'. Some girls and boys can be prone to develop anorexia nervosa in early puberty (Fisman *et al.* 1996; Gillberg and Rastam 1992). At this stage the person can be very sensitive to criticism, especially with regard to their personal appearance, social skills and attributes valued by their peers (e.g. weight).

During the hormonal changes and increased stress associated with adolescence, the teenager may have a temporary increase in their expression of Asperger's Syndrome. Parents need to be supportive and patient and remember that this is a difficult time for virtually all children. Although the physical changes of adolescents are likely to occur at the same time as other teenagers, for those with Asperger's Syndrome the emotional changes of adolescence may be significantly delayed. While other teenagers are intent on romance and testing the rules, the teenager with Asperger's Syndrome still wants simple friendships, has strong moral values and wants to achieve high grades. It is important to explain that the values and attributes of the adolescent with Asperger's Syndrome may be different to their peers', but are positive qualities not yet recognised by others. They can be ridiculed for being a prude or 'nerd'. A strong attachment to or sexual interest in someone often occurs later than usual, with adolescent qualities extending well into the person's twenties. Thus the emotional changes of adolescence are often delayed and prolonged.

16. Can the person develop normal relationships?

In early childhood, the person is often content with their own company and that of their immediate family. There may actually be a dislike of social or physical contact with others, and a preference for solitary pursuits. However, some children approach others as if they were a family member with associated greetings, close proximity and touching. They do not realise that there are different behavioural codes for the various levels of relationships. This may be embarrassing for others and lead to misinterpretation of the signals. The child can also be vulnerable to exploitation by others. They will need instruction on the different ways of relating to family, to teacher, friends and strangers. The person may not comprehend why we behave differently according to the company, but the Circle of Friends programme can provide a visual model and guidance.

The technique is very simple. Draw concentric circles, i.e. circles within circles as occurs on a dart board, on a large sheet of paper and write the name of the child in the innermost circle. Within the next circle, write the greeting and actions appropriate to the child's 'inner circle', and who would be within that circle. This is usually the child's immediate family. Appropriate actions may be kisses, cuddles and hugs. The next circle would be for the child's extended family and their close friends. Actions would be less intimate. The next circle would be for friends, teachers, etc., with subsequent circles for acquaintances or strangers. Photographs of specific individuals and actions can be placed by the child in the appropriate circles. This visual aide helps discussion of the appropriate social codes for the various levels of relationship.

Teenagers with Asperger's Syndrome can be delayed in their social/emotional maturity compared to the other children in their class. Their friendships tend to be based on common interests and intellectual pursuits rather than self–disclosure, romance and sexual discovery. Their choice of friends may also not follow the conventions of similar age and culture. The person subsequently can be teased for not being part of the 'in' group and naive in their knowledge of sexuality. They are also vulnerable to misinformation. The child can consider school programmes on human relationships and sexuality as irrelevant and boring, especially if the adolescent has not yet reached the social maturity of others in their class. Such programmes may have to be repeated to coincide with the time when the material is relevant to the individual.

When romantic relationships do occur, it is important the adolescent learns how to 'read' the signals of the other person. The person can develop an infatuation or crush on someone that is not reciprocated. This is a natural component of teenage life, but with Asperger's Syndrome there are additional features. The person may assume the other feels the same way about them and not be aware of the polite signals that indicate the relationship is one sided. Someone may need to point out these signals. The other aspect is that the person may also not be aware of the signals when someone's intentions are not romantic or friendly. The person with Asperger's Syndrome can be vulnerable to being the victim of sexual assault. The author has known several victims of rape with Asperger's Syndrome, both female and male, but to date, no offenders.

With a prolonged emotional adolescence and delayed acquisition of social skills the person may not have a close and intimate relationship until much later than their peers. Such a relationship may appear inconceivable during the teenage years, but long-term experience has indicated that not all people with Asperger's Syndrome remain socially isolated and celibate. Their partner can often share similar hobbies or career and this can be how the couple first meet.

The partner is often flattered by the intensity of the other person's dedication to them and their qualities of reliability, honesty and fidelity. The author has noted that marriage partners who do not have the same personality and interests tend to be very nurturing and protective individuals who compensate for any difficulties with the social aspects of life. However, some males with the syndrome do have considerable problems finding a partner, and travel abroad to find a someone who, due to cultural differences or financial circumstances, shows less concern about their husband's social eccentricities (Gillberg and Gillberg 1996).

One area that needs to be explored is marital and relationship counselling. From the author's clinical experience, the person with this syndrome can be confusing or infuriating for their partner. Two sources of conflict are physical and emotional intimacy and the dominance of the special interest.

For example, a husband complained that his wife, who had Asperger's Syndrome, was too cold and aloof. He said that when he was showing affection it was 'like hugging a plank of wood'. The partners may need counselling on each other's background and perspective. One could describe the relationship as similar to a marriage between two people from very different cultures, unaware of the conventions and expectations of the other partner. They unwittingly step on each other's toes. The author often uses the analogy of a person from a different culture to explain the problems experienced by the person with Asperger's Syndrome and the people they meet.

Certainly in the early courtship days parents may have to provide some explanations to boyfriends or girlfriends who are confused as to why the person is so different regarding physical intimacy and rarely uses the words and gestures of love and affection. This may also be relevant for families and younger children. For example, the mother of a teenager expressed her concern that her son with Asperger's Syndrome rarely showed any signs of love for her. He replied that he told her that he loved her when he was six years old and was confused as to why he should have to repeat those words. Surely she knew. In another example, a husband had difficulty determining when and how to say comments expressing his love for his wife. However, he could write her a letter with an eloquence and passion that was unattainable using speech. The suggestion here was to write more letters and read them to his wife.

Another source of conflict (or boredom) is the person's fascination with their special interest. At first this may be an endearing quality, but eventually it becomes annoying, especially when there may be other priorities. The other partner may have a disproportionate share of family or household responsibilities. Again, both parties need to understand the perspective of their partner. Relationship counselling can help, but the counsellor will need to understand the nature of Asperger's Syndrome.

It is important to recognise that the person with Asperger's Syndrome may have some character faults, but they are less likely to be unfaithful or squander the family budget, although their frugal nature can be another source of conflict. There can also be conflict over the person's ways of dealing with personal crises. They can avoid any discussion on contentious issues and become socially isolated for hours or days. The person is solving their problems by retreating into their own thoughts, but their partner resents being excluded. They are hurt that at such moments their opinions or ideas are not considered.

Some individuals choose celibacy. This is described by Temple Grandin (1995) in her latest autobiography:

> I've remained celibate because doing so helps me to avoid the many complicated social situations that are too difficult for me to handle. For most people with autism, physical closeness is as much a problem as not understanding basic social behaviours. At conventions I have talked to several women who were raped on dates because they did not understand the subtle cues of sexual interest. Likewise, men who want to date often don't understand how to relate to a woman. They remind me of Data, the android on *Star Trek*. In one episode, Data's attempts at dating were a disaster. When he tried to be romantic, he complimented his date

by using scientific terminology. Even very able adults with autism have such problems. (p.133)

Celibacy may be a way of avoiding emotional and physical intimacy and the pain of failed relationships. But on the way to that decision, the person may need counselling and support if they try, and fail, to have close personal relationships.

Thus, the person with Asperger's Syndrome can develop normal relationships, as the normal range is so wide. To be successful the relationship requires considerable love, tolerance and understanding from both parties.

17. Are people with Asperger's Syndrome more likely to be involved in criminal activities?

The literature on Asperger's Syndrome includes several reports of individuals who have committed criminal offences (Baron-Cohen 1988; Cooper, Mohamed and Collacott 1993; Everall and Le Couteur 1990; Mawson, Grounds and Tantam 1985), although the actual incidence of violent offences is remarkably low (Ghaziuddin, Tsai and Ghaziuddin 1991). Cases include individuals who have been brought before the criminal justice system for a variety of offences that are usually related to their special interests, sensory sensitivity or strong moral code. The author met an adult whose special interest was filling in Lotto forms. The local newsagent objected to the number of forms he completed without any intention of payment. He was subsequently banned from the newsagent's shop. Several weeks later there was a burglary at the same shop and the only items stolen were several thousand blank Lotto forms. The police had a prime suspect, and his bedroom was found to contain the missing forms. Due to the unusual nature of the offence he was referred to a forensic psychiatrist. There are other instances of people with Asperger's Syndrome being admitted to psychiatric or secure units for quite unusual crimes associated with their interest, especially if the interest is weapons, poisons or fire.

There have been cases where an offence has been committed due to sensory sensitivity. In one case the person was sensitive to the noise of dogs barking, children crying and sopranos singing. Some readers may sympathise with him, but his actions in compelling them to stop involved the police and criminal charges. There are also occasions when the person's strong moral code has led them to confront and criticise people whose clothing or behaviour is considered 'immoral' and to be charged with offensive behaviour. The courts as well as corrective and forensic services are becoming increasingly aware of the nature of Asperger's Syndrome and are responding accordingly. These incidents are rare, and parents should not be overly concerned that their son or daughter is likely to commit a criminal offence. From the author's clinical experience, such individuals are more likely to be victims than offenders. Their naivety and vulnerability make them easy targets.

18. What resources are needed?

The child with Asperger's Syndrome does not have the behavioural and learning profile of a child with classic autism, and schools or units for such children may not be an appropriate option. The child is also not acutely disturbed and psychiatric services can be reluctant to provide services for someone with a developmental disorder. The child may have specific learning problems but not be considered eligible for services for the intellectually disabled (Simblett and Wilson 1993). Thus the conventional government services often have few resources, services and policies for people with this syndrome.

First and foremost, the family and teacher need access to expertise in this area, as well as resources and programmes for specific areas of concern. A review of the research and range of resources available for people with autism has shown that the education of such children requires expertise above anything else (Newsom 1995). The same is probably true for Asperger's Syndrome. Individual members of relevant professional groups need to develop expertise in this area. For example, education departments can enable designated staff to acquire training and expertise in this area so that teachers can contact them for advice. The designated person can visit the classroom to observe the child and provide explanations, strategies, resources and inservice training. This source has proved particularly valuable in the author's home state. Should distance be a problem then modern technology can be of assistance using video recordings and telephone conferences.

There is no single professional group or agency that should have a monopoly on the diagnosis, treatment and support of children and adults with Asperger's Syndrome. They need access to a multi-disciplinary range of professionals and a variety of agencies, from speech therapists to specialised employment services. At present there is limited professional and community knowledge of this syndrome, but a catalyst to generate knowledge, understanding and services is the development of local parent support groups.

As knowledge of Asperger's Syndrome has its origins from the study of autism, the first parent support groups are likely to be subgroups of established networks for parents of autistic children. These eventually may become autonomous and provide specific resources and services. Of foremost importance is an opportunity for parents to meet families who share the same experiences and problems, helping them to feel less isolated. The group also allows an opportunity to discuss and share strategies for specific problems, provides a consumers' opinion of services, and may invite professionals to address their meeting. Such groups also become a means of informing professionals and government agencies about Asperger's Syndrome by organising conferences and workshops. They also act as a pressure group to inform the media, politicians and the community about their circumstances and the need for appropriate resources.

One of the crucial resources is access to support and tuition in the classroom, especially in the primary school. The author has found that once a particular school gains experience and a reputation for successful programmes, there is likely to be an increase in enrolments for similar children. Parents and professionals have an informal 'good school guide'.

Many of the programmes described in this book require opportunities for one-to-one tuition or small group activities. These may require the services of a teacher aide allocated to a particular child. Their role is crucial and complex but their main responsibilities are to:

- encourage the child to be sociable, flexible and cooperative when playing or working with other children
- help the child to recognise the codes of conduct
- provide tuition on feelings and friendships

- encourage conversation skills

- help the child to develop and apply special interests as a means of improving motivation, talent and knowledge

- implement a programme to improve gross and fine motor skills

- encourage the understanding of the perspectives and thoughts of others

- provide remedial tuition for specific learning problems

- enable the child to cope with their auditory or tactile sensitivity.

Thus the aide applies a programme designed by the teacher and relevant therapists and specialists that addresses behavioural, social, linguistic, motor and sensory abilities.

When one considers the resources needed for adults with a severe expression of the syndrome, it is suprising that we currently have very little information on this popultion. The National Autistic Society in London has listed some of the issues through the organisation's contacts with adults (Bebbington and Sellers 1996). Their list is as follows:

- The need to know that there are other people like themselves.

- Concern that other professionals who come into contact with them either do not recognise Asperger's Syndrome or are not fully aware of the nature of the condition.

- Feelings of isolation.

- Difficulties in getting and keeping jobs.

- If working, not given duties commensurate with ability.

- Teasing from work colleagues.

- Difficulty in coping on a low income.

Contact with local support groups and correspondence using web sites, e-mail and internet forums can reduce feelings of isolation. Several sites are included in Appendix I. As regards employment and support with accomodation and income, the West Midlands branch of the National Autistic Society has proposed the appointment of a local Community Support Practitioner (Morgan 1996). This person's role is to act as an advocate and coach regarding financial management, daily living skills and social welfare specifically for local adults with Asperger's Syndrome who need support.

19. What should we look for in a school and teacher?

The child with Asperger's Syndrome is most likely to be enrolled at a conventional rather than a special school. What are the attributes of a good school? The author has had extensive experience of observing and supporting children with Asperger's Syndrome in a wide variety of schools. The general conclusion is that certain attributes are essential, while others are of limited relevance.

The most important attributes are the personality and ability of the class teacher, and their access to support and resources. The child with Asperger's Syndrome is quite a challenge. Teachers need to have a calm disposition, be predictable in their emotional reactions, flexible with their curriculum, and see the positive side of the child. A keen sense of humour will also help. At times the child is likely to enchant them, and a moment later totally confuse them.

An interesting feature of Asperger's Syndrome is the variability in expression of the signs from day to day. On a good day the child concentrates, conforms, socialises and learns reasonably well, but on other days they seem to be self absorbed, and lack confidence and ability. It is as if the signs come in waves or a 'tide' that has a cycle internal to the child. On such days it is best to concentrate on revision of well practised and successful activities, and be patient until the tide recedes and the child can progress once more. Should this become an issue, then parents and teachers can chart the cycle and examine the internal or external factors that may influence the cycle.

It-is not essential that the teacher has experience of similar children, as each child with Asperger's Syndrome is unique, and a teacher uses different strategies for each individual. Learning how to understand and relate to each other may take several months, so one must not use how the child responds and learns in the first few weeks as an indication of how they will be throughout the year. The child is also likely to take some time to settle in to the school routine after an absence on vacation. It does not matter how old the teacher is, how big the school, or whether it is a government or private school. What is important is the size of the classroom. Open plan and noisy classrooms are best avoided. The children respond well to a quiet, well-ordered class with an atmosphere of encouragement rather than criticism. Parents find that with some teachers the child thrives, while with others the year was a disaster for both parties. If the teacher and child are compatible, then this will be reflected in the attitude of other children in the class. If the teacher is supportive then the other children will amplify this approach. If they are critical and would prefer the child were excluded, other children will adopt and express this attitude.

Another important factor (mentioned in a previous section) that encourages successful inclusion in the classroom is that the teacher has access to practical support in terms of teacher aide time and advice from specialists in this area. It is also important that the teacher has emotional and practical support from colleagues and the school administration. The teacher and school will have to make some special allowances. For example, if the child finds school assembly a challenge with its noise and having to wait, then it may be prudent to suggest that the child wait quietly in the classroom during assembly. Special allowances may have to be made for school tests and examinations when the child's performance is affected by anxiety or depression.

Once parents have located a school that provides the necessary resources, then it is important to maintain consistency. Going to a new school means changing friends and the school not being aware of the child's abilities and history of successful and unsuccessful strategies. It is inevitable that the child will have to move to high school, but this can be made easier if they transfer with friends they have known for several years, and teachers and support staff from both schools meet to discuss how to facilitate the transition. Several features of the transition have proved to be very important, namely allowing the child to visit the school several times before the new term to ensure they know the geography of the campus and routes to classes. It is also advisable to have a teacher who is allocated specific responsibility to monitor the child's adjustment to the new school.

Attending high school can present new problems. In primary school, the teacher and child are together for a year and have the time to understand each other. The atmosphere at primary school also has a supportive or maternal quality from staff and children that can more readily accommodate and tolerate the child with Asperger's Syndrome. At high school, the teachers do not have the time to devote to one child and have a more rigid curriculum. Other teenagers can also be far less tolerant.

The diagnostic signs may also be minimal at this age, and some high school teachers have no concept of this type of disability. The child is considered as simply defiant, wilfully disobedient or emotionally disturbed, and conventional discipline is assumed to be effective. To prevent potential confrontation and despair for all parties, it would help if there can be a brief inservice programme on Asperger's Syndrome for the high school, emphasising the problems faced by the child, their means of coping with frustration, change and criticism, and the qualities they can exhibit in special areas. Once they are understood and their point of view explained, teachers can accommodate their unusual behaviour in class.

Finally, parents can be concerned as to how well conventional schools can adjust and help a child with Asperger's Syndrome, and consider whether the child would be better placed in a class, unit or school exclusively for such children. A residential school has recently opened in the United Kingdom for children and adolescents with Asperger's Syndrome (Gething and Rigg 1996). Classes have a ratio of six pupils to two staff and a curriculum designed for such children. In future, parents may campaign for and achieve this alternative option for those who have considerable difficulty in coping with conventional schools.

20. What are the advantages of using the term Asperger's Syndrome?

Once parents have a diagnosis for their unusual child they can end their nomadic wandering in search of an explanation. They also know where to go to seek advice. In addition there can be intense relief at the recognition that it is a neurobiological condition and not caused by some inadequacy, abuse or neglect in the family. However, there can be some confusion if the term High Functioning Autism is used as an alternative. Although technically Asperger's Syndrome is part of the autistic continuum or spectrum, the child does not behave or have the limited range of abilities associated with the public's image of an autistic child. The term autism can be confusing, especially as such children have a relatively limited prognosis or future, often requiring extensive support. It is also important to recognise that the child with Asperger's Syndrome does not simply have a mild form of autism, but a different expression of the condition.

Unfortunately the term autism is also associated with disturbed behaviour and teachers can be apprehensive when informed that their class will include a child with High Functioning Autism. The term Asperger's Syndrome is new and does not have any negative association for the public and professionals. When a child is said to have Asperger's Syndrome, the usual response is, 'I've never heard of that. What is it?' The reply can simply explain that the child has a neurological condition which means that they are learning how to socialise and understand the thoughts and feelings of other people, have difficulty with a natural conversation, and can develop an intense fascination in a particular area of interest and be a little clumsy. These problems are best described as a combination of developmental delay and an unusual profile of abilities. Over time the child improves.

The term also has advantages for professionals. Such children and adults are a diagnostic puzzle, and professionals can be unsure where to go to seek information or advice. This is particularly important for psychiatric services where the teenager or adult is showing signs of depression, anxiety or anger. One diagnostic area that may never have been considered is the autistic continuum, as the person has clear speech, wants to be sociable and have friends and has an intellectual capacity in the normal range. They present a picture quite unlike any autistic child they may have seen during their professional training. Once individuals and agencies are aware of the nature of Asperger's Syndrome they realise how their expertise can be applied to an existing body of knowledge on the syndrome, and which organisations, colleagues and journals can be consulted for assistance.

21. How do you share the news?

Parents often ask whom they should inform about the diagnosis, how and when. The teacher and school authorities will certainly benefit from this information, as they can obtain access to resources and strategies to help the child. Should the other children in the class be informed? The answer will vary according to each child and their circumstances. For some it may help if the diagnosis becomes public knowledge, while for others it may be preferable that they are not distinguished from other children. There have been instances when the term Asperger's Syndrome has become a derogatory term to tease the child, with the name changed to 'Asparagus' Syndrome or 'Hamburger' Syndrome. The author adopts the principle of – who *needs* to know? It is important to exercise discretion with such confidential information.

How do you explain the syndrome to other children? Carol Gray (1996) has written a programme for school children called the Sixth Sense, that is, the social sense. A series of activities highlights each sense and demonstrates how the sixth sense works. They are then encouraged to imagine what it must be like to have an impaired social sense and not fully understand the perceptual, cognitive and emotional perspective of others. For example, they are asked:

○ Would it be easy or difficult to take turns if you didn't know what others are thinking or how they feel?

○ Would it be easy or difficult to talk to others about something they did?

○ Would it be easy or difficult to make friends?

Finally, the children are encouraged to identify how they might assist their classmate with Asperger's Syndrome.

Sometimes it may be necessary to explain the nature of Asperger's Syndrome to the parents of other children in the class. They can believe the child is unusual due to some parental inadequacy, or the child is a potential danger to their son or daughter. The child's parents or a professional can address the school's Parents and Citizens Association to allay their fears and to consider ways they can help the child and their family.

How do we tell their brothers and sisters? They will probably overhear conversations and somehow learn of the diagnosis. If they have a level of maturity to understand the nature of the syndrome, then they should be informed. Fortunately there is now some literature on how to inform siblings, (Davies 1994), and parent support groups have organised activities just for siblings. These are usually coordinated by an adult who is the brother or sister of someone with Asperger's

Syndrome. The sessions enable siblings to share and discuss their feelings, learn how to cope with specific situations, such as the response of their friends when they visit, and understand that feelings of embarrassment or rivalry are quite natural. They may feel burdened with an extra responsibility, especially at school, be confused as to why their parents are so concerned, wonder if their brother or sister will get better, and how they can help them.

When do you inform the child that they have Asperger's Syndrome? There is no simple answer. Very young children will not have the maturity to understand the concepts. Older children may be extremely sensitive to any suggestion that they are different. Their vehement denial of any inadequacy in social abilities is more an attempt to convince themselves than others. The answer may be to tell the child when they are emotionally able to cope with the information and want to know why they have difficulties in situations that other children find so easy. Sometimes this should be undertaken by parents, sometimes by a professional.

Carol Gray (1996a) has designed a workbook entitled *Pictures of Me*, which can be used to introduce the child to their diagnosis. The workbook is completed by the child, their parents and a professional, and involves a very positive attitude to the syndrome. The activities focus on the person's talents and abilities. The following is David's perception of his qualities:

What's Good About Me?
1. I read well.
2. I'm good on a computer – Windows.
3. I'm good at Bowling (193 highest score).
4. I have a job.
5. I'm good at Canasta and Rummie Royal.
6. I'm good at Blackjack on computer.
7. I'm good at getting my own breakfast.
8. I'm good at putting the kettle on.
9. I'm good at Maths.
10. I'm good at spelling sometimes.

(David Downie)

The author has found that their qualities of personality include being honest, loyal, reliable, forthright and having a strong moral code and sense of justice. Their cognitive qualities include an exceptional memory, enthusiasm and knowledge about their special interest, an original way of thinking, good imagination and remarkable ability to think using pictures. These qualities are not unique to the syndrome but are enhanced by it.

People with Asperger's Syndrome have many positive qualities in their abilities and personality. There are scientists and artists who have Asperger's Syndrome who have used those qualities for great achievement. It is not a condition to be ashamed of, but one to express with pride. It is also important to explain that the person will improve their social abilities and that they can achieve their goals in life. It may take some time, and Tom Allen described himself as like a tortoise, developing small steps that eventually help win the race. Others have considered an analogy of climbing a mountain, again using small steps, but ultimately reaching the top. Better late than never!

Once the person knows they have this syndrome it can provide a sense of relief and understanding. This information may not have been acquired by a planned discussion with a parent or professional, but by reading literature on the subject. Christopher Gillberg (1991) describes how a 12-year-old entered his office and by chance found a leaflet for parents on the syndrome. The child then said:

> 'This is something I've never heard anybody say a word about before. I think I'll call it A.S. for short.' On reading the text aloud he soon remarked, as though in passing: 'It seems I have A.S.! By golly, I do have A.S. Wait till my father hears about this. My parents just might have A.S. too, you know, my father in particular, he too has all-absorbing interests. Now I can tell my classmates the reason why I pace the school yard briskly ten times up and down each break all the year round is I have A.S. And it will get my teacher off my back. If you have a handicap condition they have to tolerate you.' (p.138)

22. What would be a suitable career?

During the person's last years of school the issue of which career or job to pursue becomes increasingly important. One must capitalise on the strengths of the individual, such as commitment to work, highly focused knowledge and dependability. The area of special interest may indicate prospective employment. An interest in science can lead to university qualifications and a professional occupation. Universities are renowned for their tolerance of unusual characters, especially if they show originality and dedication in their research. The comment has been made that universities are sheltered workshops for the socially challenged! Many of the great advances in science and art have been achieved by people with Asperger's Syndrome. Indeed, it is the author's opinion that our society would benefit from the greater recognition and development of their qualities.

A common career choice is engineering (Baron-Cohen *et al.* 1997), however, one must not assume that the only career options involve science, engineering and computers. The author has noted the success of individuals who have chosen a career with the caring professions, particularly as teachers, working with the elderly or with animals, and as police officers. They have a very strong moral code and fight vehemently against social injustice.

Certain work skills will have to be encouraged, especially presentation at job interviews. The person may not be a natural salesperson for their talents, or be aware of the body language and conversational script for such occasions. Employment agencies are becoming increasingly aware of the difficulties faced by someone with Asperger's Syndrome, and are providing instruction and practice in the necessary skills. It is important to increase the person's work experience from an early age, perhaps with a newspaper or leaflet delivery, and voluntary work.

The major issues regarding employment are how the person will cope with the social aspects of the job, changes in routine and expectations, and their integrity. Some jobs require good social skills. One is reminded of the problems faced by the guests of Fawlty Towers and the leisure centre run by Mr Brittas in the popular television comedy series. These occupations are best avoided. It is also best to avoid a workforce with a strong culture of social dynamics, gossip and initiation. One woman with Asperger's Syndrome had excellent qualities in caring for the geriatric patients in a hospital ward but could not cope with the skills in social cohesion necessary when the staff met at break times. She was often ridiculed or teased. However, when she started solitary visits to the elderly in their own homes, she could continue her work without having to cope with the social culture of her colleagues.

Another option is to develop skills to work on a self-employed basis. The person may work from home, or develop expertise in an area that does not require being part of a team or hierarchy. For example, the person with Asperger's Syndrome may become skilled at craft work, or designing or repairing electronic equipment and after a period of training and apprenticeship develop their own business. The author advocates the traditional vocational training model of master and apprentice as some students with Asperger's Syndrome can have difficulty with the social aspects of college based training.

The person may have problems coping with changes in emotional atmosphere or routine. One young man was quite happy working in a factory until there was a strike. He then had to resign as he could not cope with the antagonism and uncertainty. Employers also need to understand the difficulties faced by the person with Asperger's Syndrome so that their workload and work space accommodates their characteristics. The person is likely to be extremely diligent, conscientious and insistent on quality rather than quantity. They may work through their lunchbreak or into the evening to ensure the work is completed to their high standard. This may not be viewed as a commendable characteristic by fellow employees or employer. The author has known of occasions of deliberate sabotage to ensure the person is dismissed from the workforce. In another example one young man was training to be a car mechanic with a large company. He was remarkably thorough in his work. When there was the option of a quick repair that would only just last the warranty period or more work time to produce greater reliability, he chose reliability. His employer wanted a quick turnover and for the customer to have to return to buy another replacement. This conflict caused his dismissal. However, when he has his own repair shop he will have a reputation for reliability and integrity.

Finally, a rewarding job, in both emotional and financial terms, can be crucial in encouraging a successful life. Temple Grandin (1992) has developed her special interest to become a highly successful designer of livestock facilities, academic and author. She describes how:

> My life is my work. If a high-functioning autistic gets an interesting job, he or she will have a fulfilling life. I spend most Friday and Saturday nights writing papers and drawing. Almost all my social contacts are with livestock people or people interested in autism. (p.123)

Thus her job has also given her access to a social life and friends based on common interests.

23. What are the long-term outcomes?

A previous section outlined some of the problems faced during adolescence. These include having to socialise with teenagers who can be cruelly intolerant, having different interests and objectives, coping with fluctuating emotions, and gaining insight into being different. Eventually these perilous times end and the person leaves school and can take greater control of the daily routine, social contact and occupation. Some parents describe how their son or daughter never seemed to have a normal childhood, but always seemed to be a miniature adult. At last they are adults and do not have to associate with teenagers. Life is much easier.

The young adult may move into a 'granny flat' attached to the parents' house as his level of domestic and financial independence increases. When the person leaves home, there can be greater success with single person accommodation, perhaps close to the family home to maintain some emotional and practical support. The person's character may not be tolerated by other tenants. Indeed, the person may require solitude at the end of the day.

For those who have a successful outcome, the following have been some important factors :

○ a mentor, that is, a teacher, relative or professional who
understands the person and provides guidance and inspiration.

- a partner who provides support, affection and commitment to the person. They compensate for their peculiarities and camouflage their difficulties.

- Success at work or in their special interest, thus offsetting the challenges in the person's social life. Social success eventually become less important in one's life. Success is not measured by companionship but by achievement. This point is illustrated by Temple Grandin (1995):

  > I know that things are missing in my life, but I have an exciting career that occupies my every waking hour. Keeping myself busy keeps my mind off what I may be missing. Sometimes parents and professionals worry too much about the social life of an adult with autism. I make social contacts via my work. If a person develops her talents, she will have contacts with people who share her interests. (p.139)

- Eventually coming to terms with their strengths and deficits and no longer wanting to become someone they cannot be, and realising they have qualities others admire.

- A natural recovery. As much as there are late walkers or talkers, there can be late socialisers, although late can be by several decades.

There has yet to be a study of the long-term outcomes for children with this syndrome. Professionals and service agencies tend to see adults who are having problems that are conspicuous and this may lead to an overly pessimistic view of the long-term outcome. Asperger's Syndrome is a developmental disorder and eventually the person does learn to improve their ability to socialise, converse, understand the thoughts and feelings of others, and to accurately and subtly express their own thoughts and feelings. The author uses the analogy of completing a jigsaw puzzle of a thousand pieces without a picture on the box. Over time, small, isolated sections of the puzzle are completed, but the overall 'picture' is not apparent. Eventually there are sufficient 'islands' of parts of the puzzle to recognise the full picture and all the pieces fall into place. The puzzle of social behaviour is solved. The author has met many adults with Asperger's Syndrome who have described how in their late twenties or thirties they eventually managed to intellectually grasp the mechanisms of social skills. From then on the only people who knew of their condition were their family and those who knew them intimately.

We recognise the continuum of expression of autism from the silent and aloof child to the person with Asperger's Syndrome. Can children with Asperger's Syndrome progress further along the continuum? We have only just begun to explore the area of the autistic continuum between Asperger's Syndrome and the normal range. However, children with this syndrome can progress to a point where the current diagnostic criteria for Asperger's Syndrome do not adequately describe the more subtle qualities that remain.

Sula Wolff (1995) has recently written a book based on her extensive clinical and research studies that explains the 'bridge' between Asperger's Syndrome and the normal range of abilities. She uses the colloquial term 'loners' or the diagnostic term Schizoid Personality Disorder to define individuals who have a specific pattern of characteristics. They tend to be solitary and emotionally detached, yet sensitive to criticism. They do not conform to conventional social rules and have unusual metaphorical speech. They also rigidly pursue their own interests and can have an unusual fantasy life. She is understandably cautious of using the diagnostic term schizoid with its ominous overtones that imply a relationship with schizophrenia, especially since she found that few actually developed schizophrenia. Perhaps the term loner is more appropriate and less likely to be misinterpreted. The present author would agree that this area of the continuum becomes more a description of someone's personality than a clear developmental disorder. Thus, Sula Wolff has explained the potential outcome for some individuals with Asperger's Syndrome and in some cases the characteristics of their relatives who never had the degree of expression we diagnose as Asperger's Syndrome.

Although it is debatable whether such individuals should have a diagnostic label or be defined as having a personality disorder, they can be very unusal characters. Digby Tantam has used the term 'lifelong eccentricity', to describe the long-term outcome of individuals with Asperger's Syndrome (Tantam 1988). The term eccentricity is not used in a derogatory sense. In this author's opinion, they are a bright thread in the rich tapestry of life. Our civilisation would be extremely dull and sterile if we did not have and treasure people with Asperger's Syndrome.

Resource Material on Emotions and Friendships

Publications

All About Me
G. Rutman and P. Jordan
McClanahan Book Company, New York, 1992
ISBN 1-56293-174-1.

This book has a section where the child looks at the events portrayed in a picture and has to choose the face that corresponds with the relevant emotion. This is suitable for pre-school age to grade 1.

Happy and Sad, Grouchy and Glad
C. Allen and T. Brannon
A Sesame Street/Golden Press book, 1992.

The Sesame Street characters describe several emotions. Suitable for grades 1 to 2.

Mr Face
(available from Kangaroo Trading, Unit A, Building 4, 9–13 Winbourne Road, PO Box 1055, Brookvale, NSW 2100, Australia. Code KD1100.

A felt wall hanging comprises a blank face and a choice of eyes, eyebrows and mouths to enable the child to choose the components of a happy, sad or angry face. Suitable for pre-school age children.

Facial Expressions
Judius, Unit 8/182, Euston Road, Alexandria, NSW, 2015, Australia. Code DL222127.

This is a useful collection of photographs of children expressing a wide range of feelings for comprehension exercises. The child has to guess the emotion portrayed in each photograph, and can sort the faces according to the different emotions. Suitable for pre-school to grade 2 children.

Writing About Feelings
Rozanne Lanczak
Hawker Brownlow Education
235 Bay Road, Cheltenham, Victoria, 3192, Australia, 1987
ISBN 0-947326-61-8.

This is an excellent book full of activities relevant to young children with Asperger's Syndrome in the 2nd to 4th grades. The child completes specific writing and drawing assignments, open-ended follow-up activities and opportunities for the child to illustrate their work.

Feelings
Aliki Brandenberg
Pan Books Ltd, London, 1989
ISBN 0330-29408-3.

Beautifully illustrated and suitable for older primary school children.

Feelings
Crestwood Company, Milwaukee.

35 black-lined cards illustrate a wide range of emotions, facial expressions and body language.

Your Emotions
B. Moses and M. Gordon, Wayland Ltd., London, 1994
ISBN 0-7502-1403-1.

This series of picture books examines the emotions of anger, sadness, jealousy and fear in an amusing story with colourful illustrations. Each book contains notes for parents and teachers with suggestions of ways to help children deal with these emotions. Suitable for grades 1 to 3.

Learning and Caring About Ourselves
Gayle Bittinger
Warren Publishing House, Everett, Washington, 1992.

Pre-school activities on feelings.

Exploring Feelings: Activities for Young Children
Susan Neuman
Humanics Ltd, P.O. Box 7400, Atlanta, Georgia, 30309, 1994.

Activities for young children from pre-school to grade 3.

Bear Hugs for Remembering the Rules
Patty Claycomb
Warren Publishing House, Everett, Washington.

Age 3-6 years. Positive activities that remind children about social rules.

Bear Hugs for Respecting Others
Patty Claycomb
Warren Publishing House, Everett, Washington.

Age 3–6 years. Positive activities about respecting others.

Courtesy
published by Early Childhood Publications, Singapore, 1994.

Activities for pre-school children. Includes examples such as, when you knock into somebody by accident, say sorry.

What Makes Me Happy?
Catherine and Lawrence Anholt, Walker Books, London, 1994.

Each page illustrates a particular feeling such as what makes me laugh, cry, jealous, etc. The child with Asperger's Syndrome could make their own book with illustrations of circumstances that provoke each feeling.

Picture My Feelings
Learning Development Aids
Duke Street, Wisbech, Cambridgeshire, United Kingdom, 1989.

Covers specific emotions and feelings. For example, I'm worried, I'm happy…The child completes the phrase by adding their own personal information, e.g. I look forward to ___; I lose my temper when ___. This is suitable for adolescents with significant learning problems.

All My Feelings at Preschool – Nathan's Day
S. Conlin and S. Levine Friedman
Parenting Press, Seattle WA, 1991. ISBN 0-943990-60-2.

The text describes Nathan's feelings at pre-school. The book is best read aloud to the child with discussion of the feelings and illustrations.

All My Feelings at Home – Ellie's Day
S. Conlin and S. Levine Friedman
Parenting Press, Seattle WA, 1989.

As above, but emphasises feelings at home. Suitable for pre-school and grade 1 children. There is a third title in the series – 'What is a Feeling?'

Dealing with Feelings
E. Crary and J. Whitney
Parenting Press, Seattle, WA.

This is a series of six books, each on a specific feeling. The titles cover the emotions of Mad, Proud, Frustrated, Scared, Excited and Furious. Suitable for grades 2 to 4.

Proud of Our Feelings
Lindsay Leghorn
Magination Press 1995.

Written for children in early primary school.

How to Draw Cartoons
A CD-ROM for Macintosh and Windows
Diamar Interactive Corporation, Seattle, WA.

The child can create original cartoon characters that express different emotions by clicking on a choice of heads, body parts and facial features. Suitable for children (and adults).

I Want to Play
E. Crary and M. Megale
Parenting Press, Seattle, WA, 1982. ISBN 0-9602862-4-1.

A problem-solving book to help children resolve social conflicts. The text increases the child's awareness of alternatives and possible consequences of different behaviours. Suitable for grades 1 to 3.

Ellen and Penguin
C. Vulliamy
Walker Books, London, 1993.

The story of Ellen and her penguin in their search for a friend.

Making Friends: A Guide to Getting Along with People
Andrew Matthews
Media Masters, Singapore, 1990. ISBN 981-00-1953-X.

This book is ideal for the more able adolescent with Asperger's Syndrome. The author has a companion book, *Being Happy!*

Friendships, Values to Live By
S. Lee Roberts and L. Hohag
The Children's Press, Chicago, 1986.

An introduction to the concept of friendship for young primary school children.

The Care and Keeping of Friends
Nadine Westcott
American Girl Library, Wisconsin, Pleasant Company Publications, 1996.

An ideal book for young teenage girls.

Pragmatic Language Trivia for Thinking Skills
M. Ann Marquis
Communication Skills Builders, Arizona, 1990.

A game format is used to learn the pragmatic aspects of language. The questions encourage thinking about what language actually means. Suitable for teenagers.

Friendzee: A Social Skills Game
Diane A. Figula
Linguistic Systems Inc, East Moline, 1992. ISBN 1 55999 236 6.

The questions are based on social situations for children aged seven to eleven years.

Circle of Friends
James Stanfield Co
Drawer 66, P.O. Box 41058, Santa Barbara, CA. 93140.

These resources were described in Chapter 8.

Higher Functioning Adolescents and Young Adults with Autism: A Teacher's Guide
A. Fullerton, J. Stratton, P. Coyne and C. Gray
Pro-ed, Texas, 1996.
ISBN 0-89079-681-5.

An excellent guide for teachers that explains the challenges faced by high school students with high functioning autism and provides strategies and curriculum activities.

How to Start a Conversation and Make Friends
Don Gabor
Sheldon Press, London, 1983.

The art of conversation for teenagers.

Future Horizons
422 E. Lamar Blvd, Suite 106, Arlington, TX.

This publishing company specialises in literature on autism and includes the publications of Carol Gray on Social Stories and Comic Strip Conversations. They publish two Social Story books that include over 300 social stories.

Social Skills Activities for Special Children
D. Mannix
Available from Helios Therapy Resources
95 Gilles Street, Adelaide, South Australia.

142 lessons to learn appropriate social behaviour for children from age 6 to 14.

Being Happy: A Handbook for Greater Confidence and Security
Andrew Matthews
Media Masters, Singapore, 1988.

A useful book for adolescents who are feeling sad.

Why is Everybody Always Picking on Me: A Guide to Handling Bullies
Terrence Webster-Doyle
North Atlantic Books, Berkeley, CA.

Pupils with Asperger's Syndrome: Classroom Management
Special Needs Support Service
Meadgate Centre, Mascalls Way, Great Baddow, Chelmsford, U.K.

A resource and strategy manual for teachers.

Watch Me, I Can Do It
Neralie Cocks
Simon and Schuster, Australia, 1993.

Helping children overcome clumsy and uncoordinated motor skills.

The Morning News
This is a publication with regular articles on Asperger's Syndrome. The material is primarily written for teachers and parents, and Carol Gray is the editor. Subscriptions can be obtained from Jennison Public School, 2140 Bauer Road, Jennison, MI 49428.

Web Sites

The Internet and service providers have web sites and forums on Asperger's Syndrome. The following are some of the key sites.

On-line Asperger's Syndrome Information and Support - O.A.S.I.S.

This would be the best starting point and is the page of Barbara Kirby.
http://www.udel.edu/bkirby/asperger/

Asperger's Syndrome Support Network Home Page

This is an Australian-based page.
http://www.vicnet.net.au/vicnet/community/asperger

Asperger's Disorder Home Page

Prepared by Kaan R. Ozbayrak with links to other sites.
http://www.ummed.edu:8000/pub/o/ozbayrak/asperger.html

The National Autistic Society

This is the Society based in London and provides details of their services and literature.
http://www.oneworld.org/autism_uk/index.html

The Autism Channel Link

The virtual newspaper for autism.
http://www.telepath.com/canace/autism.html

Future Horizons

Publishing company of literature on autism.
http://www.onramp.net/autism/

The Centre for the Study of Autism

A useful source of information on autism, associated syndromes and research.
www.autism.org

Web Site maintained by people with autism/Asperger's Syndrome

This is an excellent site for peer support, forums, and self-help strategies.
http://amug.org/na203/index.html

Oops…Wrong Planet Syndrome.

This provides a personal and informative perspective on Asperger's Syndrome.

www.geocities.com/HotSprings/8442/index.htm

Both Compuserve and America Online have subscriber services and forums on Asperger's Syndrome.

How Do You Feel Today?

Aggressive	Anxious	Apologetic	Arrogant	Bashful
Blissful	Bored	Cautious	Cold	Confident
Curious	Determined	Disappointed	Disbelieving	Enraged
Envious	Exhausted	Frightened	Frustrated	Guilty
Happy	Horrified	Hot	Hungover	Hurt
Hysterical	Indifferent	Interested	Jealous	Lonely
Lovestruck	Negative	Regretful	Relieved	Sad
Satisfied	Surprised	Suspicious	Undecided	Other ...

(Please indicate which faces apply)
This would need to be simplified for younger children and new faces would be drawn to illustrate other feelings. The above is reproduced from *100 Training Games*, Gary Kroehnert, McGraw-Hill Book Company, Australia, Sydney, 1991.

Diagnostic Criteria

Table 1: Diagnostic criteria for Asperger's Syndrome from Gillberg and Gillberg (1989)

1. *Social impairment* (extreme egocentricity)
   (at least in two of the following):
   - (a) Inability to interact with peers
   - (b) Lack of desire to interact with peers
   - (c) Lack of appreciation of social cues
   - (d) Socially and emotionally inappropriate behaviour

2. *Narrow interest*
   (at least one of the following):
   - (a) Exclusion of other activities
   - (b) Repetitive adherence
   - (c) More rote than meaning

3. *Repetitive routines*
   (at least one of the following):
   - (a) On self, in aspects of life
   - (b) On others

4. *Speech and language peculiarities*
   (at least three of the following):
   - (a) Delayed development
   - (b) Superficially perfect expressive language
   - (c) Formal pedantic language
   - (d) Odd prosody, peculiar voice characteristics
   - (e) Impairment of comprehension including misinterpretations of literal/implied meanings

Table 1: Diagnostic criteria for Asperger's Syndrome from Gillberg and Gillberg (1989) (cont.)

5.   *Non-verbal communication problems*
     (at least one of the following):
         (a) Limited use of gestures
         (b) Clumsy/gauche body language
         (c) Limited facial expression
         (d) Inappropriate expression
         (e) Peculiar stiff gaze

6.   *Motor clumsiness*
         Poor performance on neuro-developmental examination

Table 2: Diagnostic criteria for Asperger's Syndrome from Szatmari, Bremner and Nagy (1989)

1. **Solitary**

   (at least two of the following):

   > No close friends
   >
   > Avoids others
   >
   > No interest in making friends
   >
   > A loner

2. **Impaired social interaction**

   (at least one of the following):

   > Approaches others only to have own needs met
   >
   > A clumsy social approach
   >
   > One-sided responses to peers
   >
   > Difficulty sensing feelings of others
   >
   > Detached from feelings of others

3. **Impaired Nonverbal Communication**

   (at least one of the following):

   > Limited facial expression
   >
   > Unable to read emotion from facial expression of child
   >
   > Unable to give message with the eyes
   >
   > Does not look at others
   >
   > Does not use hands to express oneself
   >
   > Gestures are large and clumsy
   >
   > Comes too close to others

4. **Odd speech**

   (at least two of the following):

   > Abnormalities in inflection
   >
   > Talks too much
   >
   > Talks too little
   >
   > Lack of cohesion to conversation
   >
   > Idiosyncratic use of words
   >
   > Repetitive patterns of speech

5. **Does not meet DSM-111-R criteria for**

   > Autistic Disorder

Table 3: Diagnostic criteria for Asperger's Disorder from DSM IV (1994)

A.   Qualitative impairment in social interaction, as manifested by at least two of the following:

   (1) marked impairment in the use of multiple nonverbal behaviours such as eye-to-eye gaze, facial expression, body postures, and gestures to regulate social interaction

   (2) failure to develop peer relationships appropriate to developmental level

   (3) a lack of spontaneous seeking to share enjoyment, interests, or achievements with other people (e.g. by a lack of showing, bringing or pointing out objects of interest to other people)

   (4) lack of social or emotional reciprocity

B.   Restricted repetitive and stereotyped patterns of behaviour, interests and activities, as manifested by at least one of the following:

   (1) encompassing preoccupation with one or more stereotyped and restricted patterns of interest that is abnormal either in intensity or focus

   (2) apparently inflexible adherence to specific, nonfunctional routines or rituals

   (3) stereotyped and repetitive motor mannerisms (e.g. hand or finger flapping or twisting, or complex whole-body movements)

   (4) persistent preoccupation with parts or objects

C.   The disturbance causes clinically significant impairment in social, occupational, or other important areas of functioning

D.   There is no clinically significant general delay in language (e.g. single words used by age 2 years, communicative phrases used by age 3 years)

Table 3: Diagnostic criteria for Asperger's Disorder
from DSM IV (1994) (cont.)

E. There is no clinically significant delay in cognitive development or in the development of age-appropriate self-help skills, adaptive behaviour (other than in social interaction), and curiosity about the environment in childhood

F. Criteria are not met for another specific Pervasive Developmental Disorder or Schizophrenia

Table 4: 'Diagnostic criteria of Asperger's Syndrome from ICD-10 (World Health Organisation, 1993)

A. There is no clinically significant general delay in spoken or receptive language or cognitive development. Diagnosis requires that single words should have developed by 2 years of age or earlier and that communicative phrases be used by 3 years of age or earlier. Self-help skills, adaptive behaviour, and curiosity about the environment during the first 3 years should be at a level consistent with normal intellectual development. However, motor milestones may be somewhat delayed and motor clumsiness is usual (although not a necessary diagnostic feature). Isolated special skills, often related to abnormal preoccupations, are common, but are not required for diagnosis.

B. Qualitative abnormalities in reciprocal social interaction are manifest in at least two of the following areas:
    (a) failure adequately to use eye-to-eye gaze, facial expression, body posture, and gesture to regulate social interaction:
    (b) failure to develop (in a manner appropriate to mental age, and despite ample opportunities) peer relationships that involve a mutual sharing of interests, activities and emotions;
    (c) lack of socio-emotional reciprocity as shown by an imparment or deviant response to other people's emotions: or lack of modulation of behaviour according to social context: or a weak integration of social, emotional and communicative behaviours;
    (d) lack of spontaneous seeking to share enjoyment, interests, or achievements with other people (e.g. a lack of showing, bringing, or pointing out to other people objects of interest to the individual).

Table 4: 'Diagnostic criteria of Asperger's Syndrome from ICD-10 (World Health Organisation, 1993) (continued)

C.   The individual exibits an unusually intense, circumscribed interest or restricted, repetitive and stereotyped patterns of behaviour, interests, and activities manifest in at least one of the following areas.

   (a)   an encompassing preoccupation with stereotyped and re-stricted patterns of interest that are abnormal in content or focus: or one or more interests that are abnormal in their intensity and circumscribed nature though not in the content or focus;

   (b)   apparently compulsive adherence to specific, non-functional routines or rituals:

   (c)   stereotyped and repetitive motor mannerisms that involve either hand/finger flapping or twisting, or complex whole body movements;

   (d)   preoccupations with part-objects or non-functional ele-ments of play materials (such as their colour, the feel of their surface, or the noise/vibration that they generate);

However it would be less usual for these to include either motor mannerisms or preoccupations with part-objects or non-functional elements of play materials.

D.   The disorder is not attributable to the other varieties of pervasive developmental disorder: simple schizophrenia, schizo-typal disorder, obsessive-compulsive disorder, anankastic personality disorder, reactive and disinhibited attachment disorders of childhood.

References

American Psychiatric Association (1994) *Diagnostic and Statistical Manual of Mental Disorders, 4th edition.* Washington, DC: American Psychiatric Association.

Anneren, G., Dahl, N., Uddenfeldt, U. and Janols, L.O. (1995) 'Asperger's Syndrome in a boy with a balanced de novo translocation'. *American Journal of Medical Genetics 56,* 330–1.

Asendorpf, J.B. (1993) 'Abnormal shyness in children.' *Journal of Child Psychology and Psychiatry 34,* 1069–1081.

Asperger, H. (1944) 'Die Autistischen Psychopathen.' In *Kindesalter, Archiv. Fur Psychiatrie und Nervenkrankheiten 117,* 76–136.

Asperger, H. (1979) 'Problems of infantile autism.' *Communication, Journal of the National Autistic Society 1979.*

Asperger, H. (1991) 'Autistic psychopathy in childhood.' In U.Frith (ed) *Autism and Asperger's Syndrome.* Cambridge: Cambridge University Press.

Attwood, A.J., Frith, V. and Hermelin, B. (1988) 'The understanding and use of interpersonal gestures by autistic and Down's Syndrome children', *Journal of Autism and Developmental Disorders 18,2,* 241–257.

Baltaxe, C.A.M., Russell, A., D'Angiola, N. and Simmons, J.Q. (1995) 'Discourse cohesion in the verbal interactions of individuals diagnosed with autistic disorder or schizotypal personality disorder.' *Australian and New Zealand Journal of Developmental Disabilities 20,* 79–96.

Barber, C. (1996) 'The integration of a very able pupil with Asperger's Syndrome into a mainstream school.' *British Journal of Special Education 23,* 19–24.

Baron-Cohen, S. (1988) 'An assessment of violence in a young man with Asperger's Syndrome.' *Journal of Child Psychology and Psychiatry 29,* 351–360.

Baron-Cohen, S. (1988a) 'Social and pragmatic deficits in autism: Cognitive or affective?' *Journal of Autism and Developmental Disorders 18*, 379–402.

Baron-Cohen, S., Campbell, R., Karmiloff-Smith, A., Grant, J. and Walker, J. (1995) 'Are children with autism blind to the mentalistic significance of the eyes?' *British Journal of Developmental Psychology 13*, 379–398.

Baron-Cohen, S. and Staunton, R. (1994) 'Do children with autism acquire the phonology of their peers? An examination of group identification through the window of bilingualism.' *First Language 14*, 241–248.

Baron-Cohen, S., Wheelwright, S., Stott, C., Bolton, P and Goodyer, I. (1997)'Is there a link between engineering and autism? *Autism, 1*, 101–109.

Barron, J. and Barron, S. (1992) *There's a Boy in Here*. New York: Simon and Schuster.

Bebbington, M. and Sellers, T. (1996) 'The needs and support of people with Asperger Syndrome'. In P. Shattock and G. Linfoot eds. *Autism on the Agenda*. London: The National Autistic Society.

Berard, G. (1993) *Hearing Equals Behaviour*. New Canaan, Conneticut: Keats Publishing.

Berthier, M.L. (1995) 'Hypomania following bereavement in Asperger's Syndrome: A case study.' *Neuropsychiatry, Neuropsychology and Behavioural Neurology 8*, 222–228.

Bettison, S. (1996) 'The long term effects of auditory training on children with autism.' *Journal of Autism and Developmental Disorders 26*, 361–374.

Bishop, D.V.M. (1989) 'Autism, Asperger's Syndrome and semantic-pragmatic disorder: Where are the boundaries?' *British Journal of Disorders of Communication 24*, 107–121.

Bolton, P., Macdonald, H., Pickles, A., Rios, P., Goode, S., Crowson, M., Bailey, A. and Rutter, M. (1994) 'A case-control family study of autism.' *Journal of Child Psychology and Psychiatry 35*, 877–900.

Bosch, G. (1970) *Infantile Autism*. New York: Springer–Verlag.

Botroff, V., Bantak,L., Langford, P., Page, M. and Tong, B. (1995) 'Social cognitive skills and implications for social skills training in adolescents with autism.' Flinders University, Adelaide, Australia. Paper presented at the 1995 National Autism Conference.

Bowler, D.M. (1992) '"Theory of Mind" in Asperger's Syndrome.' *Journal of Child Psychology and Psychiatry 33,* 877–893.

Brook, S.L. and Bowler, D.M. (1992) 'Autism by another name? Semantic and pragmatic impairments in children.' *Journal of Autism and Developmental Disorders 22,* 61–81.

Bryson, B. (1995) *Notes from a Small Island.* London: Transworld Publishers.

Burgoine, E. and Wing, L. (1983) 'Identical triplets with Asperger's Syndrome.' *British Journal of Psychiatry 143,* 261–265.

Capps, L., Yirmiya, N. and Sigman, M. (1992) 'Understanding of simple and complex emotions in non-retarded children with autism.' *Journal of Child Psychology and Psychiatry 33,* 7, 1169–1182.

Carpentieri, S.C. and Morgan, S. (1994) 'A comparison of patterns of cognitive functioning of autistic and non-autistic retarded children on the Stanford-Binet.' Fourth Edition, *Journal of Autism and Developmental Disorders 24,* 215–223.

Cesaroni, L. and Garber, M. (1991) 'Exploring the experience of autism through first hand accounts.' *Journal of Autism and Developmental Disorders 21,* 303–313.

Cooper, S.A., Mohamed, W.N. and Collacott, R.A. (1993) 'Possible Asperger's Syndrome in a mentally handicapped transvestite offender.' *Journal of Intellectual Disability Research 37,* 189–194.

Courchesne, E. (1995) 'New evidence of cerebellar and brainstem hypoplasia in autistic infants, children and adolescents.' *Journal of Autism and Developmental Disorders 25,* 19–22.

Davies, J. (1994) *Able Autistic Children – Children with Asperger's Syndrome: A Booklet for Brothers and Sisters.* Nottingham: Child Development Research Unit, University of Nottingham.

DeLong, G.R. and Dwyer, J.T. (1988) 'Correlation of family history with specific autistic subgroups: Asperger's Syndrome and Bipolar

Affective Disease.' *Journal of Autism and Developmental Disorders 18,* 593–600.

Dewey, M. (1991) 'Living with Asperger's Syndrome.' In U. Frith (ed) *Autism and Asperger's Syndrome.* Cambridge: Cambridge University Press.

Eales, M. (1993) 'Pragmatic impairments in adults with childhood diagnoses of autism, a developmental receptive language disorder.' *Journal of Autism and Developmental Disorders 23,* 593–617.

Ehlers, S. and Gillberg, C. (1993) 'The epidemiology of Asperger's Syndrome – A total population study.' *Journal of Child Psychology and Psychiatry 34,* 1327–1350.

Eisenmajer, R., Prior, M., Leekman, S., Wing, L., Gould, J., Welham, M. and Ong, B. (1996) 'Comparison of clinical symptoms in autism and Asperger's Syndrome.' *Journal of the American Academy of Child and Adolescent Psychiatry 35,* 1523–1531.

El-Badri, S.M. and Lewis, M. (1993) 'Left hemisphere and cerebellar damage in Asperger's syndrome.' *Irish Journal of Psychological Medicine 10,* 22–23.

Ellis, H.D., Ellis, D.M., Fraser, W. and Deb, S. (1994) 'A preliminary study of right hemisphere cognitive deficits and impaired social judgements among young people with Asperger Syndrome.' *European Child and Adolescent Psychiatry 3,* 255–266.

Everall, I.P. and Lecouteur, A. (1990) 'Firesetting in an adolescent boy with Asperger's Syndrome.' *British Journal of Psychiatry 157,* 284–287.

Fine, J., Bartolucci, G., Ginsberg, G. and Szatmari, P. (1991) 'The use of intonation to communicate in Pervasive Developmental Disorders.' *Journal of Child Psychology and Psychiatry 32,* 777–782.

Fisman, S., Steele, M., Short, J., Byrne, T., and Lavallee, C. (1996) 'Case study: Anorexia nervosa and autistic disorder in an adolescent girl.' *Journal of American Academy of Child and Adolescent Psychiatry 35,* 937–940.

Fletcher, P.C., Happé, F., Frith, U., Baker, S.C., Dolan, R.J., Frackowiak, R.S.J., and Frith, C.D. (1995) 'Other minds in the brain: A functional imaging study of 'theory of mind' in story comprehension.' *Cognition 57,* 109–128.

Frith, U. (1989) *Autism : Explaining the Enigma.* Oxford: Basil Blackwell Ltd.

Frith, U. (1991) 'Asperger and his syndrome.' In U. Frith (ed) *Autism and Asperger Syndrome.* Cambridge: Cambridge University Press.

Frith, U. and Happé, F. (1994) 'Autism: Beyond "Theory of Mind." *Cognition 50,* 115–132.

Garnett, M.S. and Attwood, A.J. (1995) 'The Australian Scale for Asperger's Syndrome.' Paper presented at the 1995 Australian National Autism Conference, Brisbane, Australia.

Gething, S. and Rigg, M., (1996) 'Transition to adult life : A curriculum for students with Asperger's Syndrome.' Paper presented at the 5th Congress Autism-Europe, Spain, 1996.

Ghaziuddin, M., Butler, E., Tsai, L. and Ghaziuddin, N., (1994) 'Is clumsiness a marker for Asperger's Syndrome?' *Journal of Intellectual Disability Research 38,* 519–527.

Ghaziuddin, M. and Gerstein, L. (1996) 'Pedantic speaking style differentiates Asperger's Syndrome from High Functioning Autism.' *Journal of Autism and Developmental Disorders 26,* 585–595.

Ghaziuddin, M., Leininger, L. and Tsai, L. (1995) 'Thought Disorder in Asperger Syndrome: Comparison with High Functioning Autism.' *Journal of Autism and Developmental Disorder 25,* 311–317.

Ghaziuddin, M., Shakal, J. and Tsai, L. (1995) 'Obstetric factors in Asperger Syndrome: Comparison with high-functioning autism.' *Journal of Intellectual Disability Research 39,* 538–543.

Ghaziuddin, M., Tsai, L. and Ghaziuddin, N. (1991) 'Brief report: Violence in Asperger Syndrome – A critique.' *Journal of Autism and Developmental Disorders 21,* 349–354.

Gillberg, C. (1983) 'Perceptual, motor and attentional deficits in Swedish primary school children: Some child psychiatric aspects.' *Journal of Child Psychology and Psychiatry 24,* 377–403.

Gillberg, C. (1989) 'Asperger's Syndrome in 23 Swedish children.' *Developmental Medicine and Child Neurology 31,* 520–31.

Gillberg, C. (1991) 'Clinical and neurobiological aspects of Asperger Syndrome in six family studies.' In U. Frith (ed) *Autism and Asperger Syndrome,* Cambridge: Cambridge University Press.

Gillberg, C. (1992) 'Savant-syndromet.' In R. Vejlsgaard (ed) *Medicinsk arsbok.* Munksgaard: Kopenhamn.

Gillberg, C. and Gillberg, I.C., (1989) 'Asperger syndrome – Some epidemiological considerations: A research note,' *Journal of Child Psychology and Psychiatry 30,* 631–638.

Gillberg, C., Gillberg, I.C. and Staffenburg, S. (1992) 'Siblings and parents of children with autism: A controlled population based study.' *Developmental Medicine and Child Neurology 34,* 389–398.

Gillberg, C. and Rastam, M. (1992) 'Do some cases of anorexia nervosa reflect underlying autistic-like conditions?' *Behavioural Neurology 5,* 27–32.

Gillberg, I.C. and Gillberg, C. (1996) 'Autism in immigrants: A population-based study from Swedish rural and urban areas.' *Journal of Intellectual Disability Research 40,* 24–31.

Goldstein, G., Minshew, N.J. and Siegel, D.J. (1994) 'Age differences in academic achievement in high functioning autistic individuals.' *Journal of Clinical and Experimental Neuropsychology 16,* 671–680.

Gordon, C.T., State, R.C., Nelson, J.E., Hamburger, S.D. and Rapoport, J.L. (1993) 'A double-blind comparison of clomipramine, desipramine and placebo in the treatment of autistic disorder.' *Archives of General Psychiatry 50,* 441–447.

Grandin, T. (1984) 'My experiences as an autistic child and review of related literature.' *Journal of Orthomolecular Psychiatry, 13,* 144–174.

Grandin, T. (1988) 'Teaching tips from a recovered autistic.' *Focus on Autistic Behaviour 3,* 1–8.

Grandin, T. (1990) 'Needs of High Functioning teenagers and adults with autism (tips from a recovered autistic).' *Focus on Autistic Behaviour 5,* 1–15.

Grandin, T. (1990) 'Sensory problems in autism.' Paper presented at the 1990 Annual Conference of the Autism Society of America, Buena Park, California, 1990.

Grandin, T. (1992) 'An inside view of autism.' In E. Schopler and G.B. Mesibov (eds) *High Functioning Individuals with Autism.* New York: Plenum Press.

Grandin, T. (1995) *Thinking in Pictures.* New York: Doubleday.

Gray, C. (1994) *Comic Strip Conversations.* Arlington: Future Horizons.

Gray, C. (1996) *The Sixth Sense.* Unpublished manuscript.

Gray, C. (1996a) 'Pictures of Me – Introducing students with Asperger's Syndrome to their talents, personality and diagnosis.' *The Morning News,* Fall, 1996.

Gray, C. A. (in press) 'Social stories and comic strip conversations with students with Asperger Syndrome and high functioning autism.' In E. Schopler, G.B. Mesibov and L. Kunce (eds) *Asperger's Syndrome and High Functioning Autism.* New York: Plenum Press.

Hallett, M., Lebieclausko, M., Thomas, S., Stanhope, S., Dondela, M., and Rumsey, J. (1993) 'Locomotion of autistic adults.' *Archives of Neurology 50,* 1304–1308.

Happé, F. (1991) 'The autobiographical writings of three Asperger's Syndrome adults: Problems of interpretations and implications for theory.' In U. Frith (ed) *Autism and Asperger's Syndrome.* Cambridge: Cambridge University Press.

Happé, F. (1994) *Autism: An Introduction to Psychological Theory.* London: University College of London Press.

Happé, F. (1994a) 'An advanced test of theory of mind.' *Journal of Autism and Developmental Disorders 24,* 129–154.

Happé, F., Ehlers, S., Fletcher, P., Frith, U., Johansson, M., Gillberg, C., Dolan, R., Frackowiak, R. and Frith, C. (1996) 'Theory of mind: in the brain. Evidence from a PET scan study of asperger's syndrome.' *Clinical Neuroscience and Neuropathology 8,* 197–201.

Harrison, J. and Baron-Cohen, S. (1995) 'Synaesthesia: Reconciling the subjective with the objective.' *Endeavour 19,* 157–160.

Hashimoto, *et al.* (1995) 'Development of brainstem and cerebellum in autistic patients.' *Journal of Autism and Developmental Disorders 25,* 1–18.

Hurlburt, R.T., Happé, F. and Frith, U. (1994) 'Sampling the form of inner experience in three adults with Asperger's Syndrome.' *Psychological Medicine 24,* 385–395.

Jolliffe, T., Lansdown, R. and Robinson, C. (1992) 'Autism: A personal account.' *Communication, Journal of the National Autistic Society 26,* 12–19.

Kerbeshian, J. and Burd, L. (1986) 'Asperger's syndrome and tourette syndrome: The case of the pinball wizard.' *British Journal of Psychiatry 148,* 731–736.

Kerbeshian, J., Burd, L. and Fisher, W. (1990) 'Asperger's Syndrome : To be or not to be?' *British Journal of Psychiatry 156,* 721–725.

Kerbeshian, J. and Burd, M.S. (1996) 'Case Study: Comorbidity among Tourette's Syndrome, Autistic Disorder and Bipolar Disorder.' *Journal of the American Academy of Child and Adolescent Psychiatry 35,* 681–685.

Klin, A., Volkmar, F.R., Sparrow, S.S., Cicchetti, D.V. and Rourke, B.P. (1995) 'Validity and neuropsychological characterization of Asperger Syndrome: Convergence with Nonverbal Learning Disabilities Syndrome.' *Journal of Child Psychology and Psychiatry 36,* 1127–1140.

Lanczak, R. (1987) *Writing About Feelings.* Victoria, Australia: Hawker Brownlow Education.

Le Couteur, A., Bailey, A., Goode, S., Pickles, A., Robertson, S., Gottesman, I. and Rutter, M. (1996) 'A broader phenotype of autism – The clinical spectrum in twins.' *Journal of Child Psychology and Psychiatry 37,* 785–801.

Loveland, K.A. and Tunali, B. (1991) 'Social scripts for conversational interactions in autism and Downs Syndrome.' *Journal of Autism and Developmental Disorders 21,* 177–186.

Manjiviona, J. and Prior, M. (1995) 'Comparison of Asperger's Syndrome and high-functioning autistic children on a test of motor impairment', *Journal of Autism and Developmental Disorders, 25,* 23–39.

Marriage, K.J., Gordon, V. and Brand, L. (1995) 'A social skills group for boys with Asperger's Syndrome.' *Australian and New Zealand Journal of Psychiatry 29,* 58–62.

Marriage, K., Miles, T. (1993) 'Clinical research implications of the co–occurrence of Asperger's and Tourette's Syndrome'. *Australian and New Zealand Journal of Psychiatry 27,* 666–672.

Marriage, K., Miles, T., Stokes, D. and Davey, M., (1995) 'Comparison of Asperger's Syndrome and High-Functioning Autistic children on a test of motor impairment', *Journal of Autism and Developmental Disorders, 25,* 23–39.

Matthews, A. (1990) *Making Friends: A Guide to Getting Along With People.* Singapore: Media Masters.

Maurer, R.G. and Damasio, A. (1982) 'Childhood autism from the point of view of behavioural neurology.' *Journal of Autism and Developmental Disorders 12,* 195–205.

Mawson, D., Grounds, A. and Tantam, D. (1985) 'Violence and Asperger's Syndrome: A case study'. *British Journal of Psychiatry 147,* 566–569.

McDougle, C.J., Price, L.H., and Goodman, W.K. (1990) 'Fluvoxamine treatment of coincident autistic disorder and obsessive compulsive disorder: A case report.' *Journal of Autism and Developmental Disorders 20,* 537–543.

McDougle, C.J., Price, L.H., Volkmar, F.R., Goodman, W.K., Ward-O'Brien, D., Nielsen, J., Bregman, J. and Cohen, D.J. (1992) 'Clomipramine in autism: Preliminary evidence of efficacy.' *Journal of the American Academy of Child and Adolescent Psychiatry 31,* 746–750.

McKelvey, J.R., Lambert, R., Mottson, L. and Shevell, M.I. (1995) 'Right hemisphere dysfunction in Asperger's Syndrome.' *Journal of Child Neurology 10,* 310–314.

McLennan, J.D., Lord, C. and Schopler, E. (1993) 'Sex differences in high functioning people with autism.' *Journal of Autism and Developmental Disorders 23,* 217–227.

Mesibov, G.B. (1984) 'Social skills training with verbal autistic adolescents and adults: A program model.' *Journal of Autism and Developmental Disorders 14,* 395–404.

Miedzianik, D.C. (1986) *My Autobiography.* Nottingham: Child Development Research Unit, University of Nottingham.

Minshow, N.J., Goldstein, G., Muenz, L.R. and Poyton, J. (1992) 'Neuropsychological functioning in nonmentally retarded Autistic individuals.' *Journal of Clinical and Experimental Neuropsychology 14,* 749–761.

Morgan, H. (1996) *Adults with Autism.*Cambridge: Cambridge University Press.

Newsom, E. (1985) *Services for Able Autistic People.* Nottingham: Child Development Research Unit, University of Nottingham.

Newsom, E. (1995) 'Evaluating interventions in autism: Problems and results.' National Autism Conference, Brisbane, Australia, 1995.

Ozonoff, S. and Miller, J. (1995) 'Teaching theory of mind: A new approach to social skills training for individuals with autism.' *Journal of Autism and Developmental Disorders 25,* 415–433.

Ozonoff, S., Rogers, S.J. and Pennington, B.F. (1991) 'Asperger's syndrome: evidence of an empirical distinction from high functioning autism.' *Journal of Child Psychology and Psychiatry 32,* 1107–1122.

Perkins, M. and Wolkind, S.N. (1991) 'Asperger's Syndrome: Who is being abused?' *Archives of Disease in Childhood 66,* 693–695.

Piven, J., Harper, J., Palmer, P. and Arndt, S. (1996) 'Course of behavioural change in autism: A retrospective study of high-IQ adolescents and adults.' *Journal of the American Academy of Child and Adolescent Psychiatry 35,* 523–529.

Piven, J., Palmer, P., Jacobi, D., Childress, D. and Arndt, S. (1997) 'Broader autism phenotype: Evidence from a family history study of multiple incidence autism families.' *American Journal of Psychiatry 154,* 185–190.

Prior, M. and Hoffman, W. (1990) 'Brief report: Neuropsychological testing of autistic children through an exploration with frontal lobe tests.' *Journal of Autism and Developmental Disorders 20,* 581–590.

Ratey, J. and Johnson, C. (1997) *Shadow Syndromes.*New York: Pantheon.

Realmuto, A. and August, G.J. (1991) 'Catatonia in autistic disorder: A sign of comorbidity or variable expression?' *Journal of Autism and Developmental Disorders 21,* 517–528.

Rickarby, G., Carruthers, A., Mitchell, M. (1991) 'Brief Report: Biological factors associated with Asperger's Syndrome.' *Journal of Autism and Developmental Disorders 21,* 341–8.

Rimland, B. (1990) 'Sound sensitivity in autism.' *Autism Research Review International 4,* 1 and 6.

Rimland, B. and Edelson, S.M. (1995) 'Brief report: A pilot study of Auditory Integration Training in autism.' *Journal of Autism and Developmental Disorders 25,* 61–70.

Roffey, S., Tarrant, T. and Majors, K. (1994) *Young Friends.* London: Cassell.

Rumsey, J. and Hamburger, S.D. (1988) 'Neuropsychological findings in high functioning men with infantile autism residual state.' *Journal of Clinical and Experimental Neuropsychology 10,* 201–221.

Ryan, R.M. (1992) 'Treatment–resistant chronic mental illness: Is it Asperger's Syndrome?' *Hospital and Community Psychiatry 43,* 807–811.

Saliba, J.R. and Griffiths, M. (1990) 'Brief report: Autism of the Asperger type associated with an autosomal fragile site.' *Journal of Autism and Developmental Disorders 20,* 569–575.

Schopler, E. and Mesibov, G.P. (eds) (1992) *High Functioning Individuals with Autism.* New York: Plenum Press.

Shah, A. (1988) 'Visuo-spatial islets of abilities and intellectual functioning in autism.' Unpublished Ph.D. thesis, University of London.

Shields, J., Varley, R., Broks, P. and Simpson (1996) 'Social cognition in developmental language disorders and high level autism.' *Developmental Medicine and Child Neurology 38,* 487–495.

Simblett, G.J. and Wilson, D.N. (1993) 'Asperger's Syndrome: Three cases and a discussion.' *Journal of Intellectual Disability Research 37,* 85–94.

Sinclair, J. (1992) 'Personal Essays.' In E. Schopler and F. Mesibov (eds) *High Functioning Individuals with Autism.* New York: Plenum Press.

Sverd, J. (1991) 'Tourette syndrome and autistic disorder: A significant relationship.' *American Journal of Medical Genetics 39,* 173–179.

Szabo, C.P. and Bracken, C. (1994) 'Imipramine and Asperger's letter to the editor.' *Journal of the American Academy of Child and Adolescent Psychiatry 33,* 431–432.

Szatmari, P., Archer, L., Fisman, S., Streiner, D.L. and Wilson, F. (1995) 'Asperger's Syndrome and autism: Differences in behaviour, cognition and adaptive functioning.' *Journal of the American Academy of Child and Adolescent Psychiatry 34,* 1662–1671.

Szatmari, P., Bartolucci, G. and Bremner, R (1989) 'A follow up of high functioning autistic children.' *Journal of Autism and Developmental Disorders 19,* 213–225.

Szatmari, P., Bartolucci, G. and Bremner, R (1989b) 'Asperger's Syndrome and autism: Comparison of early history and outcome.' *Developmental Medicine and Child Neurology 31,* 709–720.

Szatmari, P., Bartolucci, G., Finlayson, M. and Tuff, L. (1990) 'Asperger's Syndrome and Autism: Neurocognitive aspects.' *Journal of the American Academy of Child and Adolescent Psychiatry 29,* 130–136.

Szatmari, P., Brenner, R. and Nagy, J. (1989) 'Asperger's syndrome: A review of clinical features.' *Canadian Journal of Psychiatry 34,* 554–560.

Tantam, D. (1988) 'Lifelong eccentricity and social isolation: Asperger's Syndrome or Schizoid Personality Disorder?' *British Journal of Psychiatry 153,* 783–791.

Tantam, D., Evered, C. and Hersov, L. (1990) 'Asperger's Syndrome and Ligamentous Laxity.' *Journal of the American Academy for Child and Adolescent Psychiatry,* 892–896.

Tantam, D. (1991) 'Asperger's Syndrome in adulthood.' In U. Frith (ed) *Autism and Asperger's Syndrome.* Cambridge: Cambridge University Press.

Tantam, D., Holmes, D. and Cordess, C. (1993) 'Non–verbal expression in autism of Asperger's type.' *Journal of Autism and Developmental Disorders 23,* 111–113.

Tirosh, E. and Canby, J. (1993) 'Autism with Hyperlexia: A distinct syndrome?' *American Journal on Mental Retardation 98,* 84–92.

Vilensky, J.A., Damasio, A.R. and Maurer, R.G. (1981) 'Gait disturbances in patients with autistic behaviour: A preliminary study.' *Archives of Neurology 38*, 646–649.

Volden, J. and Loud, C. (1991) 'Neologisms and idiosyncratic language in autistic speakers.' *Journal of Autism and Developmental Disorders 21*, 109–130.

Volkmar *et al.* (1994) 'DSM IV Autism/P.D.D. field trial.' *American Journal of Psychiatry 151*, 1361–1367.

Volkmar, F.R., Klin, A., Schultz, R., Bronen, R., Marans, W.D., Sparrow, S. and Cohen, D.J. (1996) 'Asperger's Syndrome.' *Journal of the American Academy of Child and Adolescent Psychiatry 35*, 118–123.

White, B.B. and White, M.S. (1987) 'Autism from the inside.' *Medical Hypotheses 24*, 223–229.

Williams, D. (1992) *Nobody Nowhere.* London: Transworld Publishers.

Williams, D. (1994) *Somebody Somewhere.* London: Transworld Publishers.

Williams, T.A. (1989) 'Social skills group for autistic children.' *Journal of Autism and Developmental Disorders 19*, 143–155.

Wing, L. (1981) 'Asperger's Syndrome: A clinical account.' *Psychological Medicine 11*, 115–130.

Wing, L. (1992) 'Manifestations of social problems in high functioning autistic people.' In E. Schopler and G. Mesibov (eds) *High Functioning Individuals with Autism.* New York: Plenum Press.

Wing, L. and Attwood, A. (1987) 'Syndromes of autism and atypical development.' In D. Cohen and A. Donnellan (eds) *Handbook of Autism and Pervasive Developmental Disorders.* New York: John Wiley and Sons.

Wolff, S. (1991) 'Asperger's Syndrome.' *Archives of Diseases in Childhood 66*, 178–179.

Wolff, S.(1995) *Loners: The Life Path of Unusual Children.* London: Routledge.

Wolff, S. and Barlow, A. (1979) 'Schizoid personality in childhood: A comparative study of schizoid, autistic and normal children.' *Journal of Child Psychology and Psychiatry 20*, 29–46.

WHO (1989) *Tenth Revision of the International Classification of Disease* Geneva: World Health Organisation.

Yirmiya, N., Sigman, M. and Freeman, B.J. (1993) 'Comparison between diagnostic instruments for identifying high functioning children with autism.' *Journal of Autism and Developmental Disorders 24,* 281–91.

Subject Index

Author Index